# COOKING
## WITH *Lauren K*

*Healthy can be delicious,
affordable, and easy!*

GREAT AMERICAN COOKBOOK COMPETITION RUNNER UP
AS SEEN ON THE RACHAEL RAY SHOW

# LAUREN KUDLAWIEC

WORD ASSOCIATION PUBLISHERS
www.wordassociation.com
1.800.827.7903

ISBN: 978-1-63385-072-9

Library of Congress Control Number: 2015907304

*Photography by*
Julie Buck
juliebuckphotography.com

*Design by*
Jason Price

*Published by*
Word Association Publishers
205 Fifth Avenue
Tarentum, Pennsylvania 15084

www.wordassociation.com
1.800.827.7903

This book is for those who believe healthy eating is difficult, tasteless, and expensive. I hope that these recipes will change your opinion and your life.

*And Jesus said unto them, "I am the bread of life. He that cometh to me shall never hunger; and he that believeth in me shall never thirst." —John 6:35*

# TABLE OF CONTENTS

# INTRODUCTION

"I hate vegetables." "I don't have time to cook a healthy meal." "Healthy food is too expensive." As a Family and Consumer Science teacher, I frequently hear excuses for why kids—and adults—avoid a healthy diet. Starting in my small college apartment in Pittsburgh, I fell in love with cooking and baking on a budget; I was determined to make nutritious food taste good. In the years following, I started my own small business to further my passion. I also acquired my Family and Consumer Science teaching certification and landed a job at Penn Cambria High School teaching cooking and nutrition courses. Authoring a cookbook was on my mind—I had a multitude of recipes that I had crafted for my students at school—but I wasn't serious enough to dedicate the time to actually do it.

That all changed one morning in November of 2013. While drinking my morning cup of tea and catching up on my DVR'd Rachael Ray episodes, I heard about The Rachael Ray Great American Cookbook Competition. I decided to compete.

The quotes at the beginning of this introduction were the first statements in my video entry for the competition. The show reviewed my application in January of 2014, complete with a video, three recipes, and two essays. With applications from over 800 people nationwide, I barely expected a phone call, let alone the phone interview and recipe package submission that I would tackle in the next two rounds of elimination. After months of recipe writing and testing, number crunching, and nutrition calculating, I crossed my fingers and hoped for a spot in the top five.

The single most memorable phone call of my life occurred on April 1, 2014: Rachael Ray personally called and invited me to New York City to compete on her show! On April 21, I headed to New York City to compete in front of a live studio audience, multiple celebrity chef judges, and, of course, Rachael Ray. In round one Chef Jacques Pépin showed us how to make classic French omelets, which we then had to replicate. Round two was a chance for me to impress the judges with one of my own appetizer recipes, which I made for Chef Josh Capon and Lauren Purcell, editor of the Rachael Ray magazine. I succeeded! Round three involved a live demonstration of my made-over Buffalo Chicken Dip (see p. 24) for *Shark Tank*'s Lori Greiner and Rachael herself.

The final challenge didn't take place until two weeks later because it required the families of three famous chefs, Richard Blais (*Top Chef*), Scott Conant (*Chopped*), and Buddy Valastro (*The Cake Boss*), to make the dishes at home from the recipes we wrote. Unfortunately for me, Fanny Slater took the crown in this challenge, leaving me in second place. I was very disappointed, but as I boarded my train home, I pondered the amazing memories I had made and the important advice and encouragement I received during the final show. I opened a new Word document and continued my work on this very book.

Competing on *The Rachael Ray Show* ignited my determination to prove that healthy eating can be affordable, easy, and tasty. This book is my manual for that idea. As I wrote this book, I've had more and more opportunities to broadcast my ideas and recipes into the hands of my community. From live demonstrations at festivals and guest speaker opportunities, to my own column in the local newspaper and my own cooking segment on Central PA Live, the chances for me to share my excitement have expanded tenfold.

After my final challenge on *The Rachael Ray Show*, Chef Scott Conant told me, "Whatever you do, just enjoy it. That's the most important thing." I truly loved writing the recipes you will use in this cookbook, and I know my family enjoys eating the food on a daily basis! I hope you, too, enjoy making these recipes for yourself, your family, and your friends.

# LAUREN K'S TIPS FOR EATING HEALTHY ON A BUDGET

1. Pick a reasonable budget and stick to it. For example, my family budgets $150 per week for three daily meals, toiletries, and cleaning products. We rarely purchase fast food or convenience items. We go out to eat one or two times per month.

   - Get an envelope for your allotted weekly budget and use only the cash for your groceries. The simplicity of swiping a credit or debit card at the grocery store makes it easy to overspend.

   - Use a calculator to keep a running tally of your grocery costs as you put them in your cart. This helps you decide if you *really* need that extra box of cereal. It also helps you make sound decisions and forces you to read the prices of the items you are buying.

2. Plan out your meals at the beginning of the week and be a smart shopper.

   - Pick dishes that use similar ingredients for two or three meals. Use my tips for making-over leftovers. This will help you prevent food waste, making the most out of the items you buy.

   - Sift through your sale flyer to seek out meat, seafood, and produce sales, and plan your meals based on bargain items. For example, I buy fresh salmon only when it is $7.99 per pound or less. If salmon is on sale, looks like we're getting some Speedy Sugar and Spice Salmon (p. 160) that week!

   - Shop one time per week for your food items. Studies have shown that the more times you enter a grocery store, the more money you spend.

- Don't shop hungry! The hungrier you are, the more likely you are to spend money on unnecessary junk food.

- Make a list that coincides with your grocery store layout. Put produce items at the top, dry goods next, and refrigerated and freezer items last. Maintaining this order allows you to keep perishable goods refrigerated for as long as possible, maximizing the shelf life of your food.

- Use coupons, but only if the check-out price will be less than a generic brand. Coupons make for a better deal when that item is already on sale that week.

- Don't be afraid of frozen whole foods. If fresh broccoli is expensive, buy frozen broccoli instead. Frozen fish, such as tilapia, is half the cost of fresh! Avoid processed frozen foods, such as premade pancakes and TV dinners, which are pricey and loaded with excess sodium and sugar.

- If possible, leave bad shopping influences at home. For example, my husband wants to buy every snack item he sees when he tags along, and I have trouble saying no. I stick to my list more easily when he isn't with me!

3. Make your meals, follow portion sizes, and encourage people to eat your food!

- Have a standard dinner time and plan when you need to start making your meal. This helps ensure that you are hungry and will eat the meals you've planned, and it takes away the temptation to order pizza or pick up fast food. For example, I know that we're always hungry for dinner around 7 p.m., so I always have dinner started by 6:30.

- Use your most perishable items first. Ground meats, leafy vegetables, and berries will expire first, so use them early in the week to prevent spoilage.

- Use proper portions when preparing and eating. The Nutritional Information I've listed for each recipe is accurate only if you follow the recipe and serving sizes.

Resist the temptation to throw in an extra handful of cheese or an additional half pound of meat. Portion control also saves you money in the long run.

- Don't make separate meals for picky eaters. Require everyone to at least try every dish in your meal. Studies show that it can take up to seven tastes of a particular food before you start to like it. Make vegetables in different ways or with different sauces each time.

- If you have picky eaters, try to include them in the meal planning and food preparation. Allowing them to help with manageable tasks they enjoy will also instill a sense of pride in the meal once it hits the table.

# COMMON SUBSTITUTIONS

Do you have recipes at home that *you* would like to make healthier? Try out some of my substitution ideas in your kitchen. Some may change the flavor or texture slightly, but experiment for your perfect recipe.

| | |
|---|---|
| Sour cream or mayonnaise | Replace half of the amount with plain Greek yogurt or seek out light versions of those items. |
| Vegetable, corn, or canola oil | **For cooking:** Use olive oil for the entire amount.<br>**For baking:** Replace half of the amount with applesauce, pumpkin puree, or plain yogurt. |
| Butter or shortening | **For cooking:** Use olive oil for the entire amount.<br>**For baking:** Replace half of the amount with applesauce or plain Greek yogurt. In dark-colored recipes, like brownies, you can also replace the entire amount with mashed avocado. |
| Egg | Replace with 2 egg whites, 1 medium banana, or 1 tablespoon of chia seeds mixed with 3 tablespoons of hot water. |
| Sugar | Replace half of the amount with mashed banana, honey, or maple syrup. |
| All-purpose flour | Replace half of the amount with stone ground whole wheat flour OR replace the entire amount with finely ground white whole wheat flour. |
| Milk or white chocolate | Replace the entire amount with dark chocolate. |
| Bacon | Use half of the amount of bacon the recipe calls for OR replace full amount with prosciutto, Canadian bacon, or turkey bacon. |

| | |
|---|---|
| Ground beef | Replace with ground turkey, pork, or chicken. |
| Pork sausage | Replace with turkey sausage. |
| Pork butt or roast | Replace with pork tenderloin. |
| Mild cheeses such as mozzarella, provolone, Monterey Jack, Colby, or mild cheddar | Reduce the amount of cheese by half and use a sharp cheese like parmesan, Asiago, sharp cheddar, blue cheese, gorgonzola, or feta. |
| Heavy cream | **In sauces:** Replace the entire amount with regular half and half, fat-free half and half, or whole milk.<br>**In soups:** Puree a 15-ounce can of white beans in a blender with 2 cups of the soup. Add back to the soup pot. |
| Pasta | Replace with whole wheat pasta or brown rice pasta.<br>*Grain-free replacements:*<br>**For spaghetti-style pasta:** Use spaghetti squash or ribbons of zucchini in equal cup amounts.<br>**For lasagna:** Use thinly sliced zucchini, yellow squash, or eggplant.<br>**For short-cut pasta:** Cut cauliflower into florets and boil for 8 minutes. |
| White rice | Use equal amounts of brown rice, quinoa, farro, or barley. Follow package directions.<br>**For a grain-free replacement:** Use cooked cauliflower pulsed into rice-sized pieces in the food processor. |
| Ricotta cheese | Replace with cottage cheese. |
| Whole milk | Replace with low-fat or skim milk, almond milk, soy milk, or coconut milk.<br>**Note:** Almond, soy, and coconut milk may significantly alter the taste in savory recipes. They are not effective replacements for regular milk in instant pudding. |

# ACKNOWLEDGEMENTS

Although I have dreamed of creating this book for about five years now, I didn't have the determination to actually do it until I competed in The Great American Cookbook Competition hosted by *The Rachael Ray Show*. I want to thank Rachael Ray, not only for offering me the chance to compete on her show, but also for being a role model for my culinary adventures for the past ten years. I also want to thank Rebecca Soldinger, producer of *The Rachael Ray Show*, for organizing the competition along with her two colleagues, Monica McCabe Kennedy and Brittany Groth. These ladies really elevated the experience for me.

My mother, Barbara Bucci, deserves an immense amount of credit for my culinary skills and talents. She introduced me to the kitchen and laid the groundwork for my belief that every family—no matter their income or preferences—can eat a well-rounded diet. Sometimes she made vegetables that I absolutely hated (Brussels sprouts) and made me eat them anyway. Guess what? Brussels sprouts are now one of my favorite vegetables. She packed school lunches for us and put healthy meals on the table every night. She helped create, test, and review many of the recipes in this book. My father, Mark Bucci, never missed an opportunity to help with my book, whether he was tasting food or giving me worthy advice. Both of my parents instilled essential Christian values in my life and emphasized the importance of putting God and family first.

Right behind my mother is my culinary equal, my sister, Leah Bucci. We made so many memories and learned so much as we grew up together in my mother's kitchen. As a fellow lover of *Food Network*, Rachael Ray, *Cooking Light* magazine, and Pinterest, we often share ideas for making things healthy and tasty. During my preparation for *The Rachael Ray Show* and the creation of this book, she would willingly drive 90 minutes from Maryland after a hard day in the operating room to help me into the late evening hours. Thank you for all of the taste-testing, recipe timing, grocery store running, food styling, and dishwashing. I think my brother, Ian Bucci, may soon become a rival in our secret sibling kitchen competitions with his his blossoming knack for preparing protein-packed foods.

My amazing husband, Bryan—my chief taste-tester, business manager, and love of my life—played a huge role in the creation of this cookbook. It was for him that I started making food, although my early days in the kitchen did not always yield tasty results. He has always been both my biggest recipe critic and recipe promoter. I thank him for supporting me in all of my culinary endeavors, from starting my own catering and cake decorating business to taking on my own cooking segment. He also took the "spare no expense" approach to this book so that I could make decisions that would best benefit my readers. Bryan always supports me, even providing the muscles that carry my equipment into venues for cooking demonstrations. He helps me see the bigger picture and focus on what's really important in life.

Many of the recipes in this cookbook stem from original dishes from my family and friends that I've made-over. I want to thank all of my wonderful family members and great friends for their personal recipes, invaluable ideas, and support for culinary creations in years past. There are too many of you to list here, but you know who you are! Thank you to my "Taste Team," who collaborated on recipes and tried out the many dishes I made in the testing process of this book. Without your constructive comments, the recipes would not be the quality they are today.

I would like to thank photographers Caitlyn Sowers and Julie Buck for the beautiful photography featured in this book.

A big thank-you goes out to the WTAJ news station in Altoona, Pennsylvania, for their faith in my ability to provide a quality cooking segment on Central PA Live. You have made one of my life dreams come true! Thank you to Cristi Kimmel, Dawn Pellas, Danielle Negri, and Scott Pickrell for all of your support on the show.

Thank you to the *Altoona Mirror* newspaper for all of the wonderful publicity, the beginning of my column "Tasty Words," and the opportunity to write for *Blair Living* magazine. Thanks to Barb Cowan who took a chance on my literary abilities and culinary ideas.

I would like to thank my sponsor, Smithmyer's Superette, store owners Jay and Louise Smithmyer, and the wonderful staff at the store. The ingredients and food tips you provide for both my cooking show and recipe development have been such a help. I can't thank you enough.

I also want to thank my Panther family at Penn Cambria School District. Your support has meant the world to me. Thanks to the administration, school board members, my fellow teachers and staff members, students, and families. Your support during The Great American

Cookbook Competition and other culinary endeavors built my confidence and desire to help our community grow strong and healthy.

Thank you to Word Association Publishers. To Tom and Francine Costello, Kendra Williamson, and Jason Price, all of your ideas, expertise, and labor transformed my recipes in a Word document into a real cookbook. I appreciate all of your efforts to make this book a high-quality work of art.

This book would not have been possible without the nutrition calculator program on the Spark Recipes website. They offer a wonderful free program where you can calculate the nutrition of any dish you would like to make, so please give it a try for your own personal recipes. See http://recipes.sparkpeople.com/recipe-calculator to check it out.

# DIETARY KEY

 **GLUTEN FREE**
This dish does not contain wheat, rye, barley or products with wheat as an ingredient.

 **LOW CARBOHYDRATE**
This dish contains less than 10 grams of carbohydrates per serving.

 **LOW SUGAR**
This contains less than 5 grams of sugar.

 **LOW FAT**
This dish contains less than 3 grams of total fat.

 **VEGETARIAN**
This dish does not contains meat, fish or seafood.

 **VEGAN**
This dish does not contain meat, fish, seafood or any animal products.

 **DAIRY-FREE**
This dish does not contain dairy products.

# APPETIZERS

BUFFALO CHICKEN DIP WITH WHOLE WHEAT PITA CHIPS

ROASTED CAULIFLOWER DIP

SKINNY SPINACH AND ARTICHOKE DIP

HUMMUS: THREE WAYS

CLASSIC LEMON AND GARLIC HUMMUS
ROASTED RED PEPPER HUMMUS
KALAMATA OLIVE HUMMUS

FRUIT SALSA WITH CINNAMON TORTILLA CHIPS

ITALIAN SAUSAGE AND PESTO SLIDERS

TOMATO RICOTTA BRUSCHETTA

NOT YOUR UNCLE BOB'S DEVILED EGGS

PEPPERONI ROLLS

BAKED CHICKEN EGG ROLLS WITH SWEET AND SPICY SAUCE

KENNEDY SHRIMP

CAPRESE SKEWERS WITH BALSAMIC DRIZZLE

HARVEST WONTON CUPS WITH BRIE

PULLED PORK NACHOS

# BUFFALO CHICKEN DIP
## WITH WHOLE WHEAT PITA CHIPS

Buffalo Chicken Dip is a game-day mainstay in my town, but this spicy appetizer, usually paired with fried tortilla chips, is anything but "light." I've made-over the original dish with my secret weapons of cottage cheese and chicken broth to cut the fat and calories in half. The wheat pita chips and veggies are great healthy dippers. I even make this one for dinner sometimes! I earned second place on The Rachael Ray Show when I demonstrated this recipe.

**TOTAL TIME:** 40 minutes
**SERVINGS:** 16, each with about 5 tablespoons dip, and 2 chips and veggies
**TOTAL COST:** $10.75*

### NUTRITIONAL INFORMATION*

| | | |
|---|---|---|
| Calories: 153 | Sodium: 523.6mg | Sugar: 1.1g |
| Total Fat: 6.6g | Carbohydrates: 9.9g | Protein: 13.8g |
| Saturated Fat: 2.5g | Fiber:1.5g | Cholesterol: 36.9mg |

*Price and nutrition include the remainder of the head of celery, cut up for dipping.*

### INGREDIENTS

4 whole wheat pita breads, cut into 8
    triangles each
2 tablespoons olive oil, divided
Salt and pepper
1 cup onion, diced
1 cup celery, diced
3 garlic cloves, minced
24 ounces cooked chicken breast or 1½
    pound boneless skinless chicken breast,
    cut into ½-inch cubes

1 tablespoon butter
3 tablespoons whole wheat flour
½ cup chicken broth
½ cup hot sauce (I use Red Hot)
1 cup low-fat cottage cheese
4 ounces cream cheese, cubed

## DIRECTIONS

**WHOLE WHEAT PITA CHIPS:** Preheat oven to 400°F. Lay the pita chips in an even layer on a greased baking sheet. Brush the chips lightly with 1½ teaspoons of olive oil. Season with salt and pepper. Flip the chips and repeat on the second side. Bake the chips in the oven for 6–8 minutes, flipping halfway through baking. Transfer to a serving bowl while you make the Buffalo Chicken Dip.

**BUFFALO CHICKEN DIP:** Heat the remaining 1 tablespoon of olive oil in a large skillet over medium heat. Add the onions, celery, and garlic, and sauté until the vegetables are soft. Add the chicken breast to the pan and season with salt and pepper. If using raw chicken, cook until the chicken is just cooked through, about 5 minutes.

Add butter to the pan and melt into chicken mixture. Stir to cover the chicken and vegetables in butter. Sprinkle flour over the entire mixture and stir to coat. Cook for 1 minute. Stir in the chicken broth and hot sauce until the mixture begins to thicken and simmer. Add the cottage cheese and cream cheese. Heat the mixture until there are no visible bits of cream cheese remaining and the mixture is simmering. You can use the back of your spoon to smooth out the cream cheese chunks to help them melt. Remove from heat.

Serve hot with pita chips and raw veggies immediately or transfer to a Crock-Pot for party-style serving.

# ROASTED CAULIFLOWER DIP

Roasted cauliflower with garlic and onions is one of my favorite side dishes. I created this recipe when I was on a "throw stuff I have in the fridge in the food processor and see if makes a good dip" kick. It's an easy appetizer to have on hand for guests, and it tastes great hot or cold. I enjoy bringing the leftovers (if there are any!) to work and sharing with my friends, who always ask for the recipe after tasting it.

**PREP TIME:** 10 minutes    **BAKE TIME:** 20 minutes
**SERVINGS:** 8, about ¼ cup each
*TOTAL COST:* $3.82

## NUTRITIONAL INFORMATION

| | | |
|---|---|---|
| Calories: 104 | Sodium: 148.3mg | Sugar: 0.7g |
| Total Fat: 8g | Carbohydrates: 5.7g | Protein: 3.4g |
| Saturated Fat: 2.9g | Fiber: 1.7g | Cholesterol: 12.4mg |

## INGREDIENTS

½ large head of cauliflower, cut into florets
1 medium onion, sliced
3 garlic cloves, smashed and peeled
1 tablespoon olive oil
Salt and pepper to season

¼ cup parmesan cheese
¼ cup light sour cream
¼ cup light mayonnaise
2 ounces cream cheese

## DIRECTIONS

Preheat oven to 400°F. Line a rimmed baking sheet with foil and coat with cooking spray to prevent sticking. Spread the cauliflower, onions, and garlic on the pan. Toss with 1 tablespoon olive oil and season with salt and pepper. Roast for 20 minutes. Remove from oven and let cool a few minutes.

Add the cauliflower mixture, parmesan cheese, light sour cream, light mayonnaise, and cream cheese to a food processor. Pulse 10 times and then let the mixture run until a smooth dip forms. Add additional salt and pepper if desired.

Serve warm or at room temperature with pita chips, crackers, pretzels, or fresh veggies, such as carrots, cucumbers, cherry tomatoes, and sugar snap peas.

# SKINNY SPINACH AND ARTICHOKE DIP

I don't have the money or metabolism to eat spinach and artichoke dip regularly at chain restaurants, even though I love it. You can imagine what I did . . . yes, I recreated my own!  I simply thaw a package of frozen spinach, crack open a can of artichoke hearts, pull out a few things from my refrigerator, and BAM . . . Skinny Spinach and Artichoke Dip is baking in less time than it takes to watch an episode of *The King of Queens*.

**PREP TIME:** 15 minutes   **BAKE TIME:** 20 minutes
**SERVINGS:** 13, ¼ cup per serving
*TOTAL COST:* $7.31

## NUTRITIONAL INFORMATION

Calories: 110

Total Fat: 8.5g

Saturated Fat: 3.5g

Sodium: 271.4mg

Carbohydrates: 2.3g

Fiber: 0.3g

Sugar: 1.1g

Protein: 4.2g

Cholesterol: 18.3mg

## INGREDIENTS

1 package frozen chopped spinach, thawed and drained completely

14-ounce can of artichokes, drained, liquid squeezed out, and chopped

½ cup light sour cream

½ cup light mayonnaise

4 ounces cream cheese

½ cup mozzarella cheese, shredded

½ cup parmesan cheese, grated

2 garlic cloves, finely minced

Salt and pepper to season

Toasted baguette slices, pretzels, wheat thins, or raw veggies for serving.

## DIRECTIONS

Preheat oven to 375°F and coat a pie plate or an 8x8-inch oven-safe baking dish with cooking spray. In a medium mixing bowl, combine all of the ingredients. Mix with an electric mixer until thoroughly combined. Spoon the mixture into the prepared dish and press down evenly with the spoon. Bake for 20 minutes or until the dip is steaming hot.

# HUMMUS—THREE WAYS

I fell in love with hummus when I was in college in Pittsburgh, where many restaurants served different flavors of this creamy dip. I couldn't afford to eat restaurant hummus every day, so I experimented in my own kitchen using inexpensive ingredients and my food processor.  The basic hummus recipe is the Classic Lemon and Garlic Hummus, but you can put your own twist on your hummus dip, like I have with the Roasted Red Pepper Hummus and the Kalamata Olive Hummus.

## CLASSIC LEMON AND GARLIC HUMMUS

**TOTAL TIME:** 10 minutes
**SERVINGS:** 12, ¼ cup each
*TOTAL COST:* $2.94

### NUTRITIONAL INFORMATION

| | | |
|---|---|---|
| Calories: 112 | Sodium: 228mg | Sugar: 0.1g |
| Total Fat: 5.2g | Carbohydrates: 14g | Protein: 3g |
| Saturated Fat: 0.7g | Fiber: 2.7g | Cholesterol: 0mg |

### INGREDIENTS

2 15-ounce cans of chickpeas, drained
1 clove of garlic, roughly chopped
Juice of 1 lemon

¼ teaspoon salt, and more for seasoning
¼ cup olive oil

### DIRECTIONS

Place drained chickpeas, garlic, lemon juice, and salt in the food processor. Pulse 10 times to break up the mixture and then let run for 30 seconds. While the food processor is running, stream in the olive oil slowly. Stop, take the top off the food processor, and push down any chunks that are stuck to the sides of the bowl. Puree again until the mixture is smooth and creamy. If you prefer a thinner hummus, you can add an additional tablespoon or two of water or olive oil. Taste and add additional salt if needed.

Serve with whole wheat pita chips, pretzels, or raw veggies.

# ROASTED RED PEPPER HUMMUS

**ACTIVE TIME:** 13 minutes   **TOTAL TIME:** 43 minutes
**SERVINGS:** 14, ¼ cup each
*TOTAL COST:* $4.23

## NUTRITIONAL INFORMATION

Calories: 85                 Sodium: 229mg              Sugar: 0.6g

Total Fat: 2.9g              Carbohydrates: 12.7g       Protein: 2.7g

Saturated Fat: 0.4g         Fiber: 2.5g                Cholesterol: 0mg

## INGREDIENTS

1 red bell pepper, washed                2 15-ounce cans of chickpeas, drained
2 tablespoons plus 1 teaspoon olive oil,  1 clove garlic
   divided                Juice of 1 lemon
Salt and pepper to season

## DIRECTIONS

Preheat oven to 400°F. Line a rimmed baking sheet with foil. Place the red bell pepper on the baking sheet, drizzle with 1 teaspoon of olive oil, and season with salt and pepper. Rub the oil and seasonings all over the pepper. Roast for 30 minutes, remove from the oven, and let cool for 5 minutes. Once the pepper is cool enough to touch, peel off the skin, stem, and seeds, and discard. The pepper flesh should yield about ½ cup of roasted red pepper.

Place the pepper in the food processor along with the chickpeas, garlic, lemon juice, and a pinch of salt. Pulse 5 times and then puree for about 30 seconds. Open the lid of the food processor and use a spoon to scrape down any big chunks that are stuck to the side of the bowl. Put the lid back on and puree again. Pour in 2 tablespoons of olive oil slowly while the processor is running, and puree until smooth and creamy. Add additional salt if needed.

# KALAMATA OLIVE HUMMUS

**TOTAL TIME:** 10 minutes
**SERVINGS:** 12, ¼ cup each
*TOTAL COST:* $4.60

## NUTRITIONAL INFORMATION

Calories: 121

Total Fat: 5.5g

Saturated Fat: 0.4g

Sodium: 398mg

Carbohydrates: 15.3g

Fiber: 2.7g

Sugar: 0.1g

Protein: 3g

Cholesterol: 0mg

## INGREDIENTS

Follow the ingredients for the Classic Lemon Garlic Hummus, plus ½ cup pitted
Kalamata olives.

## DIRECTIONS

Place drained chickpeas, Kalamata olives, garlic, lemon juice, and salt in the food processor. Pulse 10 times to break up the mixture and then let run for 30 seconds. While the food processor is running, stream in the olive oil slowly. Stop, take the top of the food processor, and push down any chunks that are stuck to the sides of the bowl. Puree again until the mixture is smooth and creamy. Taste and add additional salt if needed.

> You can pick up small amounts of Kalamata olives at the antipasto bar of your deli instead of buying a whole jar.

# FRUIT SALSA
## WITH CINNAMON TORTILLA CHIPS

They say the fastest way to a person's heart is through their stomach. I took this recipe with me as an edible visual aid to win over the hearts of the interview panel for my teaching job at my school. Needless to say, it got me hired! Feel free to substitute some of your favorite fruits into this recipe.

**TOTAL TIME:** 35 minutes
**SERVINGS:** 10, each with 1 cup of fruit salsa and 6 chips
*TOTAL COST:* $12.33

## NUTRITIONAL INFORMATION

Calories: 136

Sodium: 142.6mg

Sugar: 12.8g

Total Fat: 1.9g

Carbohydrates: 28.9g

Protein: 2.7g

Saturated Fat: 0.6g

Fiber: 4.2g

Cholesterol: 0mg

## INGREDIENTS

**Tortilla Chips**

6 large (8–9 inch) whole wheat tortillas

2 teaspoons cinnamon

1 tablespoon sugar

Cooking spray

**Fruit Salsa**

3 cups fresh pineapple, diced (about ½ large pineapple)

2 cups diced strawberries

1 large mango, peeled and diced

2 apples or peaches, diced

3 kiwi, peeled and diced

1 cup blueberries

Juice of 1 lime

2 tablespoons sugar

2 teaspoons cinnamon

## DIRECTIONS

**TORTILLA CHIPS:** Preheat oven to 400°F. On a cutting board, cut tortillas in half and then cut into 5 wedges. Evenly spread out tortilla pieces onto a baking sheet. Combine cinnamon and sugar into a small bowl. Spray a light coating of cooking spray over the tortilla wedges. Sprinkle them with half of the cinnamon and sugar mixture. Flip them over and repeat. Bake for 6–8 minutes, turning once halfway through baking.

**FRUIT SALSA:** Add diced pineapple, strawberries, mango, apples, kiwi, and blueberries into a large serving bowl. Juice the lime over a small bowl. Add sugar and cinnamon and stir until well combined. Pour lime dressing over the fruit, and fold salsa to distribute evenly. Serve with tortilla chips.

# ITALIAN SAUSAGE AND PESTO SLIDERS

Game day always brings hungry mouths to my table. While I'm preparing my main dishes, I put these sliders out for my guests and watch them disappear! They are not only quick and cheap, but satisfying.

**PREP TIME:** 20 minutes    **BAKE TIME:** 4–5 minutes
**SERVINGS:** 15 sliders
*TOTAL COST:* $11.63

## NUTRITIONAL INFORMATION

Calories: 177
Total Fat: 7.3g
Saturated Fat: 2.9g

Sodium: 324mg
Carbohydrates: 14.8g
Fiber: 0.4g

Sugar: 1.5g
Protein: 8.3g
Cholesterol: 27mg

## INGREDIENTS

1 pound turkey sausage, casings removed
15 slider buns or small dinner rolls
⅓ cup prepared pesto (to make your own, see Poor Man's Pesto, p. 234)
3 Roma or plum tomatoes, sliced into 5 slices each
1 cup mozzarella or Italian-blend cheese, grated

## DIRECTIONS

Preheat oven to 400°F. In a medium skillet, brown the turkey sausage over medium heat, breaking it into small pieces with a wooden spoon as it cooks. Meanwhile, slice the slider buns in half, if needed, and lay them out on a rimmed baking sheet. Spread 1 teaspoon pesto on the top half of each bun. When the sausage is fully cooked, spoon about 1 heaping tablespoon of sausage onto the bottom half of each slider. Top each slider with about 1 tablespoon of cheese and one tomato slice. Bake for 4–5 minutes, or until the cheese melts. Flip the pesto-covered bun tops onto the sliders and serve hot.

# TOMATO RICOTTA BRUSCHETTA

I love the pairing of creamy Italian cheeses, fresh basil, and tomatoes. You can whip up this easy appetizer for your guests in no time, and it looks so fancy to boot! Use a baguette for small rounds or a wider loaf for larger pieces.

**TOTAL TIME:** 20 minutes
**SERVINGS:** 20, 2 small or 1 large bruschetta (large shown in picture)
*TOTAL COST:* $7.62

## NUTRITIONAL INFORMATION

| | | |
|---|---|---|
| Calories: 99 | Sodium: 207.5mg | Sugar: 1.2g |
| Total Fat: 2.5g | Carbohydrates: 14.3g | Protein: 4.9g |
| Saturated Fat: 1.1g | Fiber: 0.7g | Cholesterol: 5.4mg |

## INGREDIENTS

16-ounce loaf whole wheat bread cut into 20 slices,
    or 2 baguette loaves cut into 20 slices each
1 cup part-skim ricotta cheese
½ cup parmesan cheese, grated or shredded
2 tablespoons fresh chopped basil
¼ teaspoon garlic powder
1 tablespoon extra virgin olive oil
⅛ teaspoon salt
¼ teaspoon fresh cracked black pepper
1 pint cherry or grape tomatoes, sliced
Additional salt and pepper for garnishing

## DIRECTIONS

Lay the bread or baguette slices on a serving platter. In a medium bowl, thoroughly mix the ricotta cheese, parmesan cheese, basil, garlic powder, olive oil, salt, and pepper. Spread the cheese mixture on the bread slices. Top with tomato slices. Sprinkle a little salt and cracked black pepper on top of the tomato slices and serve.

# NOT YOUR UNCLE BOB'S DEVILED EGGS

My father-in-law, Bob, is the deviled egg master of the Kudlawiec family. However, the full cup of mayo and 12 egg yolks as two main ingredients stops me from eating more than one. He urged me to come up with a healthy version of his eggs for this book. This collaborative recipe packs a powerful flavor punch as well as some lean protein and unsaturated fat. For only 37 calories each, you gotta give 'em a try at your next party!

**TOTAL TIME:** 30 minutes
**SERVINGS:** 24 filled deviled egg halves
*TOTAL COST:* $3.60

## NUTRITIONAL INFORMATION

Calories: 37

Total Fat: 2.5g

Saturated Fat: 0.5g

Sodium: 75.7mg

Carbohydrates: 1g

Fiber: 0.1g

Sugar: 0.6g

Protein: 2.8g

Cholesterol: 46.6mg

## INGREDIENTS

12 large eggs

½ large ripe avocado

1 tablespoon lemon juice

¼ cup plain low-fat Greek yogurt

¼ cup light mayonnaise

1 teaspoon yellow mustard

1 teaspoon hot sauce

2 tablespoons sweet pickle relish

Salt and pepper for seasoning

Paprika for garnish

## DIRECTIONS

**HARD-BOILED EGGS:** Place eggs in a stock pot and cover with cold water until the water is 1 inch above the top of the eggs. Bring the water to a boil, uncovered. Let boil for 2 minutes, then remove from heat and cover. Let the eggs sit in the hot water for 10 minutes. Use a slotted spoon to

This is Rachael Ray's recipe for hard-boiled eggs. It works perfectly every time!

remove the eggs from the water into a bowl filled with ice water. Let cool completely and then peel. Cut each egg in half. Save 6 yolks for use in filling, and discard the remaining yolks.

**FILLING:** While the eggs cook, prepare the filling. In a medium mixing bowl, mash the avocado with a fork until creamy. Add the lemon juice to prevent browning and mix thoroughly. Add the Greek yogurt, light mayonnaise, yellow mustard, hot sauce, and sweet pickle relish. Mix with a hand mixer until thoroughly combined. Add the 6 egg yolks to the bowl. Break up the yolks with a fork and combine with the other filling ingredients with the mixer. Season to taste with salt and pepper. Use small spoon to distribute the filling among the 24 egg halves, about one tablespoon in each. Sprinkle a few dashes of paprika on each egg for garnish. Keep refrigerated until serving.

Out of sweet pickle relish? Finely chop bread and butter pickles or dill pickles to get 2 tablespoons chopped pickle. Mix in ½ teaspoon sugar.

# PEPPERONI ROLLS

When I coached track and field, there were two snacks my athletes always requested I bring to our meets: my chocolate chip cookies (see p. 208) and these pepperoni rolls. I must give credit to my friend, Adrienne Berardi, for this recipe—she shared this amazing appetizer with me years ago, and now I'm passing it on to you.

**PREP TIME:** 30 minutes     **BAKE TIME:** 15–18 minutes
**SERVINGS:** 36 rolls
*TOTAL COST:* $12.05

## NUTRITIONAL INFORMATION

| | | |
|---|---|---|
| Calories: 130 | Sodium: 340.8mg | Sugar: 2g |
| Total Fat: 3.3g | Carbohydrates: 19.2g | Protein: 5.4g |
| Saturated Fat: 0.8g | Fiber: 1.1g | Cholesterol: 17.6mg |

## INGREDIENTS

36 frozen dinner rolls, such as Rhodes
2 5-ounce packages sliced turkey pepperoni, about 170 slices
¾ cup shredded parmesan cheese
1 tablespoon + 1 teaspoon dried Italian herbs, such as oregano, basil or parsley
1 egg, beaten

## DIRECTIONS

Preheat oven to 200°F. Spray 2 large rimmed baking sheets with cooking spray. Lay out 18 frozen rolls on each baking sheet with space between each roll. Once the oven reaches 200°F, shut the oven off and place the rolls in the oven to thaw. Remove the rolls after 15 minutes. They should be completely thawed.

Preheat oven to 400°F. Wipe down a large area of your counter. Using your fingers, spread each dough ball into a round disk about 3–4 inches wide. Top each disk with a pinch (about 1 teaspoon) of cheese. Sprinkle herbs on top of the cheese. Top with 4 slices of pepperoni. Take the outside edges of the dough and fold towards the middle and pinch, creating a purse. Place the rolls on the baking sheet, pinched side down, 18 rolls per sheet.

In a small bowl, beat the egg with the remaining 1 teaspoon of dried herbs. Brush the egg mixture onto the rolls with a basting brush. Bake for 15–18 minutes or until golden brown. Serve hot or at room temperature.

**MORE FILLINGS:**
You can fill these rolls with anything—ham and cheese, sundried tomato and pesto, or buffalo chicken. Make them sweet by spooning in chocolate hazelnut spread and peanut butter.

# BAKED CHICKEN EGG ROLLS
## WITH SWEET AND SPICY SAUCE

I always enjoy biting into a warm egg roll, but all of the grease and fat never sit well with my stomach afterwards. My made-over egg rolls are healthier and less greasy than your typical egg roll, and they are simple to prepare. They make an impressive and tasty appetizer for any meal!

**PREP TIME:** 45 minutes   **BAKE TIME:** 18–20 minutes
**SERVINGS:** 20, 1 egg roll and 1 tablespoon of sauce each
*TOTAL COST:* $15.04

### NUTRITIONAL INFORMATION *per Egg Roll*

| | | |
|---|---|---|
| Calories: 150 | Sodium: 375.7mg | Sugar: 0.7g |
| Total Fat: 1.9g | Carbohydrates: 22.2g | Protein: 11.2g |
| Saturated Fat: 0.2g | Fiber: 1.8g | Cholesterol: 22.9mg |

### NUTRITIONAL INFORMATION *per Tablespoon of Sauce*

| | | |
|---|---|---|
| Calories: 33 | Sodium: 170.1mg | Sugar: 2.4g |
| Total Fat: 2.2g | Carbohydrates: 2.9g | Protein: 0.6g |
| Saturated Fat: 0.3g | Fiber: 0.1g | Cholesterol: 0mg |

### INGREDIENTS
**Egg Rolls**

4 teaspoons sesame oil, divided
1 small onion, finely chopped
3 garlic cloves, minced
16-ounce bag coleslaw mix (or 7 cups of raw cabbage, shredded)
10 ounces (roughly 3 cups) shredded carrots

3½ cups cooked chicken breast, diced
2 tablespoons soy sauce
6 green onions, finely chopped (about ½ cup)
Olive oil cooking spray
20 egg roll wrappers, such as Frieda's

**Sweet and Spicy Sauce**

½ cup orange juice

2 tablespoons honey

2 tablespoons natural peanut butter

1 tablespoon fish sauce

2 tablespoons rice wine vinegar

2 tablespoons soy sauce

2 tablespoons sesame oil

1 teaspoon Sriracha chili sauce (more if you want a spicier sauce)

## DIRECTIONS

**EGG ROLLS:** Heat 2 teaspoons of sesame oil in a large skillet over medium heat. Add onions and garlic and sauté for about 3 minutes, or until onions are translucent. Add in cabbage and carrots and cook, stirring every few minutes. Meanwhile, dice the chicken. After the vegetables are soft (about 5–7 minutes), add chicken to skillet and heat through. Drizzle in the soy sauce and the remaining 2 teaspoons of sesame oil. Sprinkle in the chopped green onions, stir the mixture together, and cook until steaming. Remove from heat and let cool enough for you to handle the filling with your hands.

Preheat oven to 400°F while you fill the egg rolls. Line 2 large baking sheets with foil and spray with olive oil spray. Fill a bowl with about 1 cup of water for sealing the egg rolls. As you fill the egg rolls, keep the unfilled wrappers covered with a tea towel to keep them from drying out.

**STEP 1:** Lay out a few egg roll wrappers at a time and place about ½ cup filling in the middle of each wrapper. With your index finger or a small basting brush, trace the outside perimeter of your egg roll wrapper with thin layer of water. This will create a seal when you are done rolling.

**STEP 2:** Gently fold the top corner over the filling. Then fold in the left and right corners towards the center.

**STEP 3:** Roll the filled wrapper toward the last corner to create a rectangular roll. The roll should be relatively tight, but the wrapper should not be stretched.

Lay each roll, seam side down, on the prepared baking sheet. Keep the filled egg rolls covered with another tea towel as you fill the rest.

Spray rolls lightly with olive oil spray. Bake uncovered for 18–20 minutes, flipping once halfway through, until rolls are golden. While they bake, make the Sweet and Spicy Sauce. Let the egg rolls cool for 5 minutes and serve with the warm sauce.

**SWEET AND SPICY SAUCE:** Combine all the sauce ingredients in a small microwavable bowl. Heat the mixture in the microwave on high for 2 minutes. Remove and whisk together to combine the sauce. Serve in a shallow bowl with your egg rolls.

# KENNEDY SHRIMP

My college friend John Meehan reminds me of a blonde version of JFK, especially when he wears his Sperrys and New England-style outfits. He once brought an appetizer to a gathering that was one of the best bites I've ever tasted. His bacon-wrapped shrimp basted with BBQ sauce were inhaled by everyone at the party in about 5 minutes. This four-ingredient version of that appetizer brings back memories of fun times with college friends.

**PREP TIME:** 20 minutes    **BAKE TIME:** 9–10 minutes
**SERVINGS:** about 27 appetizers
**TOTAL COST:** $10.73

## NUTRITIONAL INFORMATION

| | | |
|---|---|---|
| Calories: 29 | Sodium: 80.1mg | Sugar: 1.2g |
| Total Fat: 0.9g | Carbohydrates: 1.4g | Protein: 3.6g |
| Saturated Fat: 0.3g | Fiber: 0g | Cholesterol: 21.4mg |

## INGREDIENTS

12 ounces raw large shrimp, peeled, deveined, and tails removed
½ pound low-sodium center-cut bacon, about 9 slices
¼ cup Sweet Garlic BBQ Sauce (see p. 237) or your favorite BBQ sauce
Fresh cracked black pepper for seasoning
27 toothpicks

## DIRECTIONS

Preheat oven to 450°F. Line a large rimmed baking sheet with foil and lay a cooling rack over the baking sheet to create a roasting rack. Coat with cooking spray. Cut the bacon slices in thirds. Wrap each shrimp in 1 of the bacon pieces and secure with a toothpick. Lay the bacon-wrapped shrimp bites on the rack with at least ½ inch of space between each piece. Baste the shrimp with the BBQ sauce and season with fresh cracked black pepper. Bake for 9–10 minutes or until the bacon is bubbly and crispy and the shrimp is fully pink. Remove cooked pieces and place on a serving platter. Serve immediately.

# CAPRESE SKEWERS
## WITH BALSAMIC DRIZZLE

These little Italian skewers are the perfect easy appetizer that can be made in a flash. With only four ingredients, these tasty bites will become your go-to potluck party dish for both you and your guests.

**TOTAL TIME:** 10 minutes
**SERVINGS:** 30 skewers
*TOTAL COST:* $7.97

### NUTRITIONAL INFORMATION

Calories: 21.6

Total Fat: 1.5g

Saturated Fat: 0.5g

Sodium: 22.7mg

Carbohydrates: 1.1g

Fiber: 0.1g

Sugar: 0.7g

Protein: 1.0g

Cholesterol: 2.7mg

### INGREDIENTS

4-ounce ball of fresh mozzarella

1 pint cherry or grape tomatoes

30 toothpicks

¼ cup pesto (see Poor Man's Pesto, p. 234)

¼ cup good-quality balsamic vinegar

### DIRECTIONS

Cut the ball of mozzarella into 60 small pieces. Skewer 2 pieces of mozzarella and 1 tomato, alternating, on each toothpick. Heat the pesto in the microwave for 10 seconds or until runny. Drizzle the pesto and then the balsamic vinegar over the skewers and serve.

# HARVEST WONTON CUPS
## WITH BRIE

On occasion, I serve multiple appetizers instead of a large meal. This appetizer was inspired by my Harvest Stuffed Acorn Squash entrée (see p. 146). These wonton cups are perfect for entertaining and will wow your guests with both amazing taste and presentation. The brie cheese and fresh parsley bring all of these secretly healthy ingredients together beautifully.

**ACTIVE TIME:** 35 minutes   **BAKE TIME:** 1 hour
**SERVINGS:** 48 appetizers
**TOTAL COST:** $13.46

### NUTRITIONAL INFORMATION

Calories: 80
Total Fat: 3.8g
Saturated Fat: 1.2g

Sodium: 154.1mg
Carbohydrates: 8.5g
Fiber: 0.7g

Sugar: 2g
Protein: 3.8g
Cholesterol: 12.8mg

### INGREDIENTS

1 medium acorn squash (about 4 inches in diameter or 2 pounds)
1 tablespoon plus 1 teaspoon olive oil, divided
Salt and pepper to taste
48 wonton wrappers (there are usually 48–52 in 1 package)
1 medium onion, chopped
1 pound turkey sausage, casings removed
2 medium golden delicious apples, cut into ½-inch cubes
½ cup sweetened dried cranberries
½ cup 99% fat free chicken broth
½ cup walnuts or pecans, roughly chopped
2 tablespoons maple syrup
1 tablespoon balsamic vinegar
8 ounces brie cheese, cut into ½-inch squares, rind removed
½ cup fresh parsley leaves, finely chopped

## DIRECTIONS

Preheat oven to 400°F.

**SQUASH (FOR FILLING):** Line a rimmed baking sheet with foil and spray with cooking spray to prevent sticking. Cut the acorn squash in half through the stem. Remove the seeds with a sturdy spoon. Drizzle ½ teaspoon of olive oil into each squash and season with salt and pepper. Spread the olive oil, salt, and pepper around the inside and outside fleshy edge of the squash with your fingers. Lay cut side down and roast for 40–45 minutes. Remove from oven and let cool for about 5 minutes.

**WONTON WRAPPERS:** Meanwhile, line 2 muffin pans with 24 wonton wrappers. Gently press the wrappers into the muffin tins to create a cup shape. Bake the cups for 4 minutes on the other rack in your oven (while the squash is baking).  Remove from oven, let cool enough to handle, and remove the baked wonton wrappers from the muffin tins. Repeat with the second batch of 24 wonton wrappers, but keep these wrappers in the muffin tins after baking.

**FILLING:** While the squash cooks, heat 1 tablespoon of olive oil in a large skillet over medium heat. Add onions and sauté for about 3 minutes. Add the turkey sausage to the cooking onions, breaking up the chunks of sausage into small pieces with the back of a wooden spoon. Cook until the sausage is browned and the onions are translucent, about 5 more minutes. Add the apples, cranberries, and chicken broth to the sausage and simmer for about 3 minutes, until the mixture begins to thicken. Add the nuts, maple syrup, and balsamic vinegar. Stir to combine and cook for about 1 minute longer. Season with salt and pepper and remove from heat. When the acorn squash is cooked, scoop out the squash from the skin, cut into ½-inch cubes, and fold into the sausage filling.

Fill the 24 wonton cups that are already in the muffin tin with about 2 tablespoons of filling. Top each with a piece of brie cheese. Bake for 5–7 minutes, until the filling is hot and the cheese is melted. Transfer finished wonton cups to a serving platter. Repeat for the second batch of pre-baked wonton cups. When all of the wonton cups are finished, garnish each with parsley and serve warm or at room temperature.

# PULLED PORK NACHOS

The Altoona Curve baseball stadium that my husband and I frequent with our friends, Stephanie and Paul Rossman, has the most amazing pulled pork nachos. I made-over a more health-conscious version of those nachos with homemade pulled pork, baked tortilla chips, and some veggie toppers. Our friends gave them the double thumbs up!

**TOTAL TIME:** 20 minutes (using cooked shredded pork)
**SERVINGS:** 6 dinner servings
**TOTAL COST:** $11.53

> **SAVE** $4.33 by using leftover pork from Crock-Pot Pulled Pork BBQ Sandwiches, p. 128!

## NUTRITIONAL INFORMATION

Calories: 486
Total Fat: 25.3g
Saturated Fat: 10.2g

Sodium: 469.5mg
Carbohydrates: 25.7g
Fiber: 2.6g

Sugar: 2.4g
Protein: 32.7g
Cholesterol: 100mg

*Price and nutrition do not include optional toppers.

## INGREDIENTS

12 small soft corn tortillas
2 tablespoon olive oil
Salt and pepper to season
2 cups pulled pork, chicken, or turkey

8-ounce block of sharp cheddar, grated
½ cup chopped green onions
Optional toppers:* Salsa, lettuce, light sour
    cream, avocado

> **Freshly grated cheese melts better and saves money.**

## DIRECTIONS

Preheat oven to 400°F. Line 2 baking sheets with foil. For the chips, cut each corn tortilla into 8 triangle wedges. Lay in an even layer over the 2 baking sheets (about 50 chips per sheet). Brush with 1 tablespoon olive oil on the first side of the chips and season with salt and pepper. Flip the chips and repeat. Bake the chips for about 6–8 minutes until the chips are crispy.

When the chips are finished, move them closer together on the baking sheets. Distribute the pulled pork and cheddar cheese evenly over the chips on both baking sheets. Bake about 8 minutes or until cheese is melted and pork is warmed.

Remove from oven and top with green onions, lettuce, salsa, sour cream, and/or avocado. I like to put out extra salsa and sour cream for dipping if desired. Serve hot.

## VARIATIONS:

For the following variations, follow the directions above using the ingredients below.

### STEELERS FAN CHICKEN NACHOS

2 cups pulled chicken, 1 cup drained and rinsed black beans, 1 cup corn, 8 ounces shredded Colby Jack cheese, and ¼ cup fresh parsley

### PHILLY STEAK AND CHEESE NACHOS

2 cups shredded beef, 8 ounces shredded provolone or pepper jack cheese, 1 cup sautéed onions and peppers

# BREAKFAST

ABE BREAKFAST WRAPS

MEAT-LOVERS OVEN FRITTATA

BROCCOLI AND FETA CRUSTLESS QUICHE

EVERYTHING BAGELS *WITH SMOKED SALMON AND DILLED CREAM CHEESE*

BERRIES-AND-CREAM CREPE SUZETTES

FLAG DAY PARFAITS

PUMPKIN GRANOLA PARFAITS *WITH FRESH PEARS*

CRANBERRY ALMOND GRANOLA

NUTTY APPLE PANCAKES

BIG BANANA PANCAKE

CINNAMON ROLL OATMEAL

PUMPKIN PIE OATMEAL

CHOCOLATE PEANUT BUTTER CUP OATMEAL

APPLE PIE OATMEAL

MIXED BERRY SMOOTHIES

APPLE PIE SMOOTHIES

# ABE BREAKFAST WRAPS

**A**vocado, **B**acon, and **E**ggs are the stars of this wrap, and what an amazing trio they make! Bacon usually gets a bad rap for being unhealthy, but you can still have its great flavor by using just a small amount. I make these wraps for my husband and me for on-the-go breakfasts.

**PREP TIME:** 20 minutes
**SERVINGS:** 4 wraps
*TOTAL COST:* $5.89

## NUTRITIONAL INFORMATION

Calories: 295

Sodium: 513 mg

Sugar: 0.9g

Total Fat: 15.6g

Carbohydrates: 21.9g

Protein: 20.7g

Saturated Fat: 3.3g

Fiber: 5.3g

Cholesterol: 196mg

## INGREDIENTS

4 slices of bacon
4 eggs plus 4 egg whites
Salt and pepper to season
1 ripe avocado
4 whole wheat wraps, thin pita breads, or tortillas (around 100 calories each)

## DIRECTIONS

Preheat oven to 350°F. Cook the bacon slices in a medium-sized skillet over medium heat until crisp. Place on a plate lined with paper towel to drain.

Heat a small skillet over medium heat. In a small mixing bowl, use a fork to beat 1 egg, 1 egg white, and a pinch of salt and pepper. Spray the skillet with cooking spray and pour the beaten eggs into the pan. Cook until eggs are set, about 2 minutes. Gently flip the egg over to cook the other side for about 30 more seconds. Repeat this procedure with the remaining eggs until you have 4 egg "pancakes."

Lay out pitas on a baking sheet. Cut the avocado in half with a knife and use your knife to remove the seed. Cut each half into 2 pieces. Use a butter knife to spread each pita with 1 of the quarters of avocado. Bake pitas for 2 minutes, just to warm them through. Remove from the oven. Crumble 1 slice of bacon onto the avocado on each pita. Top each with an egg pancake. Roll up and enjoy!

### ACE BREAKFAST WRAPS

Replace the bacon with ½ cup cheese. Sprinkle 2 tablespoons of cheese on top of the mashed avocado on each pita, bake for 3 minutes, and top with the egg pancake. This is a great vegetarian wrap.

### PIZZA BREAKFAST WRAPS

Yes . . . you can have pizza for breakfast! Replace the avocado with ½ cup of tomato sauce and the bacon for ½ cup Italian cheese. Spread 2 tablespoons tomato sauce onto each pita and top with 2 tablespoons cheese. Bake for 3 minutes or until the cheese is melted. Top with egg pancake and roll it up for a breakfast pizza on the go.

# MEAT-LOVERS OVEN FRITTATA

According to the men in my family, a big weekend breakfast isn't complete without sausage and bacon. This frittata leaves the normal pie crust behind and replaces it with tons of meaty flavor that will keep any guy, or gal, satisfied through lunch!

**PREP TIME:** 15 minutes    **BAKE TIME:** 35–40 minutes
**SERVINGS:** 8 slices
*TOTAL COST:* $4.49

## NUTRITIONAL INFORMATION

Calories: 150            Sodium: 465mg            Sugar: 1.8g
Total Fat: 9.3g          Carbohydrates: 2g        Protein: 14g
Saturated Fat: 3g        Fiber: 0g                Cholesterol: 211.1mg

## INGREDIENTS

2 links of sweet Italian turkey sausage (about 6 ounces)
3 slices of bacon
17 slices turkey pepperoni, chopped
8 eggs
1 cup low-fat milk
Salt and pepper

## DIRECTIONS

Preheat oven to 375°F and spray a pie plate with cooking spray. Heat a medium-sized skillet over medium heat. Remove the casing from the turkey sausage if needed and crumble into the pan. Use a wooden spoon to break sausage into small pieces, and sauté until browned. Spread evenly in the bottom of the pie plate. In the same skillet, fry bacon until crispy. Chop and sprinkle evenly over the sausage. Sprinkle the chopped pepperoni over the sausage and bacon.

In a medium bowl, beat eggs and milk with a fork until well combined. Season with salt and pepper and beat again. Gently pour the egg mixture over the cooked meats in the pie plate. Bake for 35–40 minutes or until the frittata is fully set and a knife inserted comes out clean. Serve hot for breakfast, lunch, or dinner.

# BROCCOLI AND FETA CRUSTLESS QUICHE

I love to make omelets, but usually I don't have time to make a full breakfast before work. This dish is great for making the night before and baking in the morning as you get ready for your day. Feel free to mix and match your own veggies and cheeses to your liking!

**PREP TIME:** 10 minutes    **BAKE TIME:** 35–40 minutes
**SERVINGS:** 8 slices
*TOTAL COST:* $4.01

## NUTRITIONAL INFORMATION

Calories: 117                    Sodium: 268.2mg                    Sugar: 1.9g
Total Fat: 7.2g                  Carbohydrates: 3.7g                Protein: 9.4g
Saturated Fat: 3.2g              Fiber: 0.8g                        Cholesterol: 195.8mg

## INGREDIENTS

3 cups steamed broccoli florets or 1 12-ounce bag of frozen broccoli florets, completely thawed
8 eggs
1 cup low-fat milk
3 green onions, roughly chopped (about ¼ cup)
Salt and pepper to season
½ cup feta cheese, crumbled

## DIRECTIONS

Preheat oven to 375°F and coat a large 10-inch pie plate with olive oil spray. Spread broccoli florets evenly around the bottom of the pie plate. In a medium bowl, beat eggs, milk, and green onions with a fork until well combined. Season with salt and pepper, add feta cheese, and whisk with the fork again. Gently pour the egg mixture over the broccoli and bake for 35–40 minutes or until the quiche is fully set and a knife inserted comes out clean. Serve with your favorite breakfast bread and fresh fruit for a complete breakfast.

# EVERYTHING BAGELS
## WITH SMOKED SALMON AND DILLED CREAM CHEESE

I fell in love with smoked salmon-topped bagels on my honeymoon, but buying one of these expensive breakfast sandwiches in Pittsburgh would put me back about $6 and 600 calories before 9:00 a.m. These made-over bagels cost $1/5$ of the price and cut out 400 calories from the usual bakery sandwich. If the cost and calorie savings don't immediately knock your socks off, the first bite sure will!

**TOTAL TIME:** 12 minutes
**SERVINGS:** 5, 2 bagel halves each
**TOTAL COST:** $11.84

**NUTRITIONAL INFORMATION**

| | | |
|---|---|---|
| Calories: 194 | Sodium: 756.2mg | Sugar: 4.7g |
| Total Fat: 6g | Carbohydrates: 25.8g | Protein: 10.8g |
| Saturated Fat: 2.6g | Fiber: 5.1g | Cholesterol: 21.2mg |

**INGREDIENTS**

4 ounces light cream cheese, softened
1 green onion, finely chopped
1 tablespoon fresh dill, roughly chopped
5 Everything Bagel Thins, such as Thomas' Bagel Thins
4 ounces smoked salmon ($6.99–$7.99 per package)

**Cinnamon Raisin Walnut Bagels:** Mix the light cream cheese with 1 teaspoon cinnamon, 1 tablespoon brown sugar, and 2 tablespoons finely chopped walnuts. Spread on cinnamon raisin bagel thins and top with sliced apples.

**DIRECTIONS**

In a small mixing bowl, combine the light cream cheese, chopped green onion, and chopped dill. Stir with a sturdy spoon until the green onion and dill are evenly distributed. Spread about 1 tablespoon of the cream cheese mixture onto each bagel thin. Top bagels evenly with pieces of the smoked salmon and serve with a side of fruit, such as berries or orange slices.

# BERRIES-AND-CREAM CREPE SUZETTES

My childhood babysitter, Jean McClemens, fostered my hobby of picking berries in the summertime. Strawberries, black raspberries, and blackberries covered our hands in pink juice as we picked and ate the delicious fruit. Today, I enjoy visiting local orchards and farmers markets to buy fresh fruits for my berry version of the traditional crepes my Grammy often made.

**COOK TIME:** 12 minutes    **TOTAL TIME:** 25–30 minutes

**SERVINGS:** 6, each with 1 crepe, 2 tablespoons cream filling, and ½ cup berries

*TOTAL COST:* $5.78

## NUTRITIONAL INFORMATION

Calories: 195

Total Fat: 7.2g

Saturated Fat: 2.8g

Sodium: 144mg

Carbohydrates: 20.8g

Fiber: 2g

Sugar: 13.7g

Protein: 11.1g

Cholesterol: 194mg

## INGREDIENTS

### Filling

3 cups fresh berries

2 ounces light cream cheese, softened

½ cup plain low-fat Greek yogurt

2 tablespoons maple syrup

½ teaspoon cinnamon

½ teaspoon vanilla

### Crepes

6 eggs

¾ cup low-fat milk

⅓ cup flour

1 tablespoon sugar

## DIRECTIONS

**FILLING:** Wash berries. If using strawberries, slice them. Set aside. In a medium mixing bowl use an electric hand mixer to mix together the cream cheese, Greek yogurt, maple syrup, cinnamon, and vanilla until smooth and creamy. Set aside while you make the crepes.

**CREPES:** Preheat a small skillet over medium-low heat. In another medium mixing bowl, whisk together the eggs, milk, flour, and sugar until well combined. Spray the skillet with non-stick spray and ladle about ⅓ cup batter into the skillet. (Use a ⅓ cup dry measuring cup for an accurate and easy pour.) Turn the skillet to coat the whole skillet with a thin layer of batter. Cook for 1 minute or until the crepe looks dry around the edges and no runny batter remains. Gently flip with a spatula and cook for an additional 30 seconds on the second side. Remove from the pan and repeat the process with the remaining batter. You should have enough batter to make 6 crepes.

Spread 2 tablespoons of the cream filling on each crepe and top with ½ cup of berries. Fold the ends of the crepe in and secure with a toothpick. If desired, add additional syrup or powdered sugar.

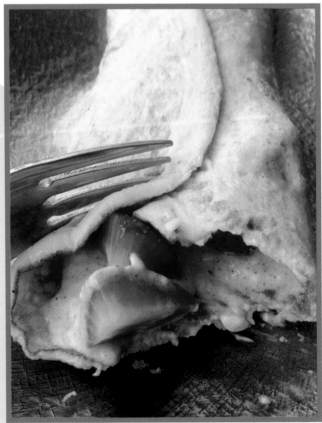

## OTHER FILLING OPTIONS

**PEACHES AND CREAM:** Use sweet cream filling above, and substitute 3 cups sliced peaches for the berries.

**CREAMSICLE:** Use sweet cream filling above, and substitute 3 cups orange or Clementine segments for the berries.

**PEANUT BUTTER CUP FILLING:** Blend 1 ounce light cream cheese, 2 tablespoons peanut butter, 1 tablespoon cocoa powder, and 2 tablespoons brown sugar for the filling. Omit the berries.

# FLAG DAY PARFAITS

Layering summer berries with yogurt and homemade granola is a great way to get three food groups into one cup. If you have already-prepared granola on hand, that works perfectly in these layered beauties as well. These patriotic cups are dedicated to Izeke Pinkas, MA2 in the U.S. Navy, and his wife (and my best friend), Erin. These two people love America as much as I love food. Cheers to this happy couple, the USA, and these Flag Day Parfaits!

**PREP TIME:** 15 minutes   **BAKE TIME:** 20 minutes
**SERVINGS:** 8 parfaits
*TOTAL COST:* $10.57

## NUTRITIONAL INFORMATION

Calories: 241         Sodium: 53.5mg        Sugar: 20.4g
Total Fat: 3.4g       Carbohydrates: 39.4g  Protein: 14g
Saturated Fat: 0.1g   Fiber: 4.6g           Cholesterol: 0mg

## INGREDIENTS

*Granola Layer*

2 cups rolled oats                     1 tablespoon vegetable or canola oil
¼ cup orange or apple juice            1 teaspoon cinnamon
¼ cup pure maple syrup

*Other Layers*

4 cups low-fat vanilla Greek yogurt (or a yogurt of your choosing)
2 cups blueberries
2 cups strawberries or raspberries

## DIRECTIONS

**GRANOLA:** Preheat oven to 375°F and coat a large rimmed baking sheet with cooking spray. Put oats in a large mixing bowl and set aside. In a small microwave-safe bowl, combine the orange or apple juice, maple syrup, vegetable oil, and cinnamon. Stir to combine, and microwave for 1 minute to dissolve the sugar. Pour mixture over the oats and toss to coat the oats completely. Spread the oat mixture on the baking sheet in an even layer. Bake for 20 minutes, stirring halfway through. Remove from the oven and cool completely.

**PARFAITS:** Layer the blueberries, yogurt, raspberries or strawberries, and granola into 12-ounce clear serving cups. Repeat the process until your parfait cups are full. Each parfait should have about ½ cup yogurt, ½ cup berries, and ¼ cup granola total. Enjoy immediately or refrigerate until serving.

# PUMPKIN GRANOLA PARFAITS
## *WITH FRESH PEARS*

My mother, Barb Bucci, is the master of holiday entertaining. She somehow finds the energy to house and host dozens of family members during Thanksgiving week. Breakfast is tough to pull together with a lot of people each day. This dish features leftover pumpkin puree, make-ahead granola, and pears from the fruit basket someone always brings to our family meal. It's a perfect breakfast for guests who are waking up and eating at different times.

**PREP TIME:** 10 minutes   **BAKE TIME:** 23–25 minutes
**SERVINGS:** 8 parfaits, each with ¼ cup granola, ½ cup yogurt, and ½ cup pears
*TOTAL COST:* $9.39

### NUTRITIONAL INFORMATION

| | | |
|---|---|---|
| Calories: 273 | Sodium: 39.6mg | Sugar: 19.4 g |
| Total Fat: 8.0g | Carbohydrates: 41.7g | Protein: 12.5g |
| Saturated Fat: 0.5g | Fiber: 5.8g | Cholesterol: 7.5mg |

### INGREDIENTS

*Granola*

| | |
|---|---|
| 2 cups old fashioned oats | 3 tablespoons maple syrup |
| ¼ cup pecans or walnuts, chopped | 2 tablespoons vegetable oil |
| ¼ cup apple juice or cider | 1 ½ teaspoons pumpkin pie spice |

*Other Layers*

| | |
|---|---|
| 32-ounce container of nonfat vanilla Greek yogurt | 1 ½ teaspoons pumpkin pie spice |
| ½ cup pumpkin puree | 4 medium pears, peeled and diced |

### DIRECTIONS

Preheat oven to 350°F. In a medium mixing bowl, combine the oats and pecans. In a small microwavable-safe bowl, combine the apple juice, maple syrup, vegetable oil, and 1½ teaspoons pumpkin pie spice. Stir to combine, and microwave for 45 seconds or until warm. Pour the mixture over the oats and pecans and toss to coat completely. Spread evenly onto a greased rimmed baking sheet. Bake for 23–25 minutes or until golden, stirring every 10 minutes. Let cool for 5 minutes and then place into a serving bowl.

While the granola bakes, pour the vanilla yogurt in a medium serving bowl. Stir in the pumpkin puree and remaining 1½ teaspoons pumpkin pie spice until well combined. Place diced pears in a separate serving bowl.

Layer the parfaits yourself or let your guests help themselves.

# CRANBERRY ALMOND GRANOLA

I created this particular recipe when a student of mine, Mitchell Mauer, brought me some fresh maple syrup straight from the tree. This granola recipe allows you to use whole ingredients, which not only saves money, but is much healthier for you, too!

**PREP TIME:** 10 minutes  **BAKE TIME:** 20 minutes
**SERVINGS:** 24, ¼ cup each
**TOTAL COST:** $6.55

### NUTRITIONAL INFORMATION

Calories: 111
Total Fat: 3.9g
Saturated Fat: 1.1g

Sodium: 1mg
Carbohydrates: 18.3g
Fiber: 2.1g

Sugar: 7.7g
Protein: 2.4g
Cholesterol: 0mg

### INGREDIENTS

4 cups rolled oats
½ cup orange or apple juice
¼ cup pure maple syrup
2 tablespoons brown sugar
2 tablespoons vegetable or canola oil

1 teaspoon cinnamon
¼ teaspoon nutmeg
¾ cup sliced or slivered almonds
1 cup sweetened dried cranberries

### DIRECTIONS

Preheat oven to 375°F and coat a large rimmed baking sheet with cooking spray. Put oats in a large mixing bowl and set aside. In a small microwave-safe bowl, combine the orange or apple juice, maple syrup, brown sugar, oil, cinnamon, and nutmeg. Stir to combine and microwave for 1 minute to dissolve the sugar. Pour mixture over the oats and toss well to coat the oats completely. Add the almonds to the oat mixture and toss to coat again. Spread the oat mixture on the baking sheet in an even layer. Bake for 20 minutes, stirring halfway through baking. Remove from oven and fold in cranberries. Cool completely before serving or storing. Store in airtight container or sealed bag for up to 2 weeks.

# NUTTY APPLE PANCAKES

My grandfather used get up at 6 a.m. to make pancakes similar to these when the grandkids stayed overnight. If you expected any to be left, you had to get up really early. I showed my students how to make these pancakes in my Basic Foods class and one student, Joshua Hayes, labeled them "nut-tastic" because he enjoyed them so much. Serve these hotcakes with a side of fresh fruit or eggs for the perfect weekend morning plate.

**PREP TIME:** 20 minutes    **COOK TIME:** 5–6 minutes per batch
**SERVINGS:** 10, 2 pancakes each
**TOTAL COST:** $6.22

## NUTRITIONAL INFORMATION

Calories: 239

Sodium: 532.9mg

Sugar: 15.3g

Total Fat: 10g

Carbohydrates: 33.3g

Protein: 7.7g

Saturated Fat: 1.2g

Fiber: 3.5g

Cholesterol: 38.9mg

## INGREDIENTS

2 cups finely-ground whole wheat flour or
   all-purpose flour
½ cup sugar
2 teaspoons baking powder
1 teaspoon baking soda
1 teaspoon ground cinnamon
½ teaspoon salt
¼ teaspoon nutmeg
2 eggs

1 ¾ cups buttermilk (or you can add 2 tablespoons
    of vinegar or lemon juice to your liquid
    measuring cup and fill up to the 1 ¾ line with
    regular milk)
3 tablespoons oil
1 ¾ cups shredded peeled apples (about 2 large)
½ cup chopped walnuts or pecans

## DIRECTIONS

In a large bowl, mix the wheat flour, sugar, baking powder, baking soda, cinnamon, salt, and nutmeg. In another bowl, whisk the eggs, buttermilk, and oil until blended. Add to flour mixture and whisk until there are no remaining lumps of flour. Whisk in the shredded apple and nuts.

Heat griddle (or a flat sauté pan) over medium-low heat. Coat the griddle lightly with cooking spray. Using a ¼-cup measure, pour dollops of pancake batter onto the griddle about 2 inches apart. Cook until bubbles break on the surface of the pancakes, about 3 minutes, and then flip gently with a spatula. Cook 1–2 more minutes or until golden brown. Serve with maple syrup or my favorite—peanut butter with cinnamon and sugar.

## LEFTOVER TIPS

These will keep and reheat very well for a few days if refrigerated. Simply place in an even layer on a microwave-safe plate and heat on high for 30–45 seconds.

**MOBILE PB&J BREAKFAST:** Smear 2 teaspoons of peanut butter and 2 teaspoons of jelly on a leftover pancake, and top with an additional pancake. This makes for a satisfying and filling on-the-go sandwich packed with whole grains, fruit, and protein. Place in plastic sandwich baggies for easy transport.

# BIG BANANA PANCAKE

No flour! No added sugar! No measuring! This recipe is so easy! Usually it's a great quick breakfast for me, but I must admit that I make this for dinner from time to time because I love it so much. See the 100-calorie topping suggestions to make your giant pancake even more scrumptious.

**TOTAL TIME:** 7 minutes
**SERVINGS:** 1 giant pancake
**TOTAL COST:** $0.87

## NUTRITIONAL INFORMATION

Calories: 228

Sodium: 182.8mg

Sugar: 17.3g

Total Fat: 5.5g

Carbohydrates: 32g

Protein: 15g

Saturated Fat: 1.8g

Fiber: 3.5g

Cholesterol: 186mg

## INGREDIENTS

1 large ripe banana, mashed

1 egg

2 egg whites

A few shakes of cinnamon (about ⅛ teaspoon)

A dash of vanilla (about ¼ teaspoon)

## DIRECTIONS

Mash the banana in a small bowl. Add the egg, egg whites, cinnamon, and vanilla to the mashed banana and beat with a fork until well combined.

Heat an 8 or 10-inch skillet over medium-low heat and coat it with cooking spray. Pour the banana-egg batter into the pan and cook until completely set, about 4 minutes. There should be no runny batter before you flip the pancake, or it will fall apart. Flip with an extra-large spatula and cook for another minute. Serve hot with your favorite pancake topping, or see my 100-calorie topper ideas.

# 100-CALORIE TOPPERS

1. **TRADITIONAL SYRUP AND BUTTER:** 1 tablespoon maple syrup and ½ tablespoon butter

2. **ALMOND SPICE:** 1 tablespoon almond butter, ½ teaspoon sugar, and a sprinkle of cinnamon

3. **CHOCOLATE PEANUT BUTTER:** ½ tablespoon natural peanut butter and ½ tablespoon Nutella

4. **PEANUT BUTTER AND JELLY:** ½ tablespoon natural peanut butter and 1 tablespoon jelly

5. **WHITE CHOCOLATE COCONUT:** 1 tablespoon white chocolate chips and 1 tablespoon shredded coconut

6. **STRAWBERRIES AND CREAM:** ½ cup chopped strawberries and ¼ cup light whipped topping

# CINNAMON ROLL OATMEAL

This recipe takes all of the wonderful flavors of a cinnamon bun and infuses them into a bowl of piping hot oatmeal. With the plump raisins and swirls of brown sugar, cinnamon, and vanilla, you'll be licking your spoon clean after every bite. This dish is so healthy and affordable, you could eat it every morning if you wanted!

**TOTAL TIME:** 12 minutes

**SERVINGS:** 4, about 1 ¼ cups each

**TOTAL COST:** $2.03

## NUTRITIONAL INFORMATION

| | | |
|---|---|---|
| Calories: 268 | Sodium: 32.3mg | Sugar: 25.8g |
| Total Fat: 3.7g | Carbohydrates: 56.2g | Protein: 7.7g |
| Saturated Fat: 0.9g | Fiber: 5.1g | Cholesterol: 3mg |

## INGREDIENTS

| | | |
|---|---|---|
| 3 cups water | ½ cup raisins | Optional: add 1–2 packets of |
| 1 cup low-fat milk or original almond milk | 1 teaspoon cinnamon | stevia or Truvia if you like it sweeter |
| 2 cups old fashioned oats | 1 teaspoon vanilla | |
| | 2 tablespoons brown sugar | |

## DIRECTIONS

In a medium or large saucepan, bring water and milk to a boil. Stir in oats and raisins, reduce heat, and simmer, stirring frequently, until the oats and raisins absorb most of the water, about 5 minutes. Stir in the cinnamon, vanilla, and brown sugar, cover, and let sit for 2 minutes. Pour into bowls and serve hot.

### MAKE-AHEAD BREAKFAST

If there are only one or two of you eating this oatmeal, make the entire recipe and place 2 or 3 portions into microwave-safe food storage containers and refrigerate. The next day, pour a splash of milk on top of the chilled oatmeal and reheat for 1 minute. Stir in the milk to make it creamy again, and enjoy.

# PUMPKIN PIE OATMEAL

I love to enjoy fall flavors, such as pumpkin, at any meal in the autumn months. With its silky texture, this warm breakfast bowl will surely help you welcome the holidays in your home.

**TOTAL TIME:** 12 minutes
**SERVINGS:** 4, about 1 ¼ cups each
*TOTAL COST:* $3.43

## NUTRITIONAL INFORMATION

Calories: 250
Total Fat: 3.9g
Saturated Fat: 0.4g

Sodium: 30.9mg
Carbohydrates: 48.2g
Fiber: 6.6g

Sugar: 19.6g
Protein: 8.1g
Cholesterol: 3mg

## INGREDIENTS

3 cups water
1 cup low-fat milk or original almond milk
2 cups old fashioned oats
1 cup pumpkin puree
1 teaspoon pumpkin pie spice
1 teaspoon vanilla
¼ cup maple syrup
Optional: add 1–2 packets of stevia or Truvia if you like it sweeter

## DIRECTIONS

In a medium or large saucepan, bring water and milk to a simmer. Stir in oats and cook for about 3 minutes, stirring frequently to prevent burning. Stir in the pumpkin puree and simmer for an additional 2 minutes. Stir in the pumpkin pie spice, vanilla, and maple syrup. Cover and let sit for 2 minutes so that most of the liquid is absorbed. Pour into bowls and serve hot.

# CHOCOLATE PEANUT BUTTER CUP OATMEAL

**TOTAL TIME:** 10 minutes

**SERVINGS:** 4, about 1 heaping cup each

**TOTAL COST:** $1.28

## NUTRITIONAL INFORMATION

Calories: 255

Total Fat: 7.8g

Saturated Fat: 1.2g

Sodium: 50mg

Carbohydrates: 42.1g

Fiber: 4.9g

Sugar: 14.3g

Protein: 9.1g

Cholesterol: 3mg

## INGREDIENTS

3 cups water

1 cup low-fat milk or original almond milk

2 cups old fashioned oats

2 tablespoons natural peanut butter

1 tablespoon cocoa powder

1 teaspoon vanilla

2 tablespoons brown sugar

Optional: add 1–2 packets of stevia or Truvia if you like it sweeter

## DIRECTIONS

In a medium or large saucepan, bring water and milk to a simmer. Stir in oats and cook for about 4 minutes, stirring frequently to prevent burning. Stir in peanut butter, cocoa powder, vanilla, and brown sugar. Cover and let sit for 2 minutes so that most of the liquid is absorbed. Pour into bowls and serve hot.

*also if using almond milk*

# APPLE PIE OATMEAL

**TOTAL TIME:** 15 minutes
**SERVINGS:** 4, about 1 ¼ cups each
**TOTAL COST:** $3.25

## NUTRITIONAL INFORMATION

Calories: 252

Total Fat: 3.7g

Saturated Fat: 0.4g

Sodium: 31.3mg

Carbohydrates: 53.3g

Fiber: 6g

Sugar: 24.6g

Protein: 7.2g

Cholesterol: 3mg

## INGREDIENTS

3 cups water

1 cup low-fat milk or original almond milk

2 cups old fashioned oats

2 cups chopped peeled apples

1 ½ teaspoons cinnamon

1 teaspoon vanilla

3 tablespoons brown sugar

Optional: add 1–2 packets of stevia or Truvia if you like it sweeter

## DIRECTIONS

In a medium or large saucepan, bring water and milk to a boil. Stir in oats and apples and simmer for about 4 minutes, stirring frequently to prevent burning. Stir in cinnamon, vanilla, and brown sugar. Cover and let sit for 2 minutes so that most of the liquid is absorbed. Pour into bowls and serve hot.

# MIXED BERRY SMOOTHIES

Two young ladies from my Basic Foods class, Tiffani Wilk and Amanda Skura, decided to do a smoothie taste-test for a class project to see if the class could detect spinach hidden in a smoothie. No one could tell the difference . . . and teenagers are always honest when it comes to food flavors! The berries in this smoothie conceal the spinach taste and color. Together, the berries and leafy greens make for a delicious and vitamin-packed treat.

**PREP TIME:** 5 minutes
**SERVINGS:** 4, 1 cup each
*TOTAL COST:* $4.90

## NUTRITIONAL INFORMATION

| | | |
|---|---|---|
| Calories: 96 | Sodium: 93.1mg | Sugar: 10.8g |
| Total Fat: 1g | Carbohydrates: 14.5g | Protein: 6.7g |
| Saturated Fat: 0g | Fiber: 2.6g | Cholesterol: 0mg |

## INGREDIENTS

2 cups ice

1 ½ cups low-fat milk or almond milk

1 ½ cup frozen mixed berries

1 cup packed fresh spinach or kale

1 cup low-fat vanilla Greek yogurt

2 packets of stevia or Truvia

½ teaspoon vanilla

## DIRECTIONS

Layer ingredients in the order shown above in your blender. Pulse on the Ice-Crush setting 10 times and then let the mixture blend for about 1 minute, or until completely blended. Scrape down sides and lid with a spoon and blend again if needed. Serve immediately.

## FUN TIPS

- Buy berries in season and freeze them in a single layer on a baking sheet. Transfer to a freezer bag and use for the next few months in your smoothies.
- Add a scoop of banana or vanilla protein powder to your ingredients for a great post-workout smoothie.

# APPLE PIE SMOOTHIES

During the winter months, I drink a lot of hot beverages, but once the summer emerges, I break out the smoothies! This one is certainly a lawn chair favorite for my family.

**TOTAL TIME:** 15 minutes
**SERVINGS:** 4, about 1 cup each
**TOTAL COST:** $3.08

### NUTRITIONAL INFORMATION

Calories: 126
Total Fat: 0.8g
Saturated Fat: 0.4g

Sodium: 46.9mg
Carbohydrates: 28.4g
Fiber: 2.7g

Sugar: 23.4g
Protein: 5.3g
Cholesterol: 5mg

### INGREDIENTS

2 large apples, peeled and sliced
½ teaspoon cinnamon, divided
1 tablespoon brown sugar
1 cup low-fat milk or almond milk

2 cups ice cubes
6-ounce container of low-fat vanilla Greek
  yogurt (roughly ¾ cup)
2 tablespoons maple syrup

### DIRECTIONS

Peel and slice apple and place in a medium bowl. Toss apple slices with ¼ teaspoon cinnamon and 1 tablespoon brown sugar. Cover tightly with plastic wrap and microwave for 3 minutes. Remove from the microwave, uncover and let cool for a few minutes. Pour in 1 cup of cold milk to further cool down apples.

In a blender, layer ice cubes, vanilla Greek yogurt, apple-milk mixture, maple syrup, and the remaining ¼ teaspoon cinnamon. Use the Ice-Crush setting and pulse 7 times and then run the blender until the mixture reaches a smooth consistency, about 30–60 seconds. Pour into glasses and garnish with a dash of cinnamon and an apple slice if desired.

## MIX IT UP!

**PROTEIN SMOOTHIE:** Add 1 scoop of vanilla protein powder to increase the protein content.
**CHOCOLATE COVERED BANANA:** In the blender, layer 2 cups ice cubes, 6 ounces vanilla Greek yogurt, 2 medium bananas, and 1 cup dark chocolate almond milk. Blend and enjoy!

# BREADS

# HONEY OATMEAL BREAD

When I was young, my favorite breakfast was hot tea and toast. This hearty whole wheat bread tastes great in the morning, or compliments most lunch and dinner meals.

**PREP TIME:** 20 minutes
**RISE TIME:** 45 minutes
**BAKE TIME:** 25–30 minutes
**MAKES:** 2 loaves   **SERVINGS:** 24 slices
**TOTAL COST:** $3.48

## NUTRITIONAL INFORMATION

Calories: 115
Total Fat: 1.2g
Saturated Fat: 0.1g

Sodium: 49.1mg
Carbohydrates: 16.9g
Fiber: 3.5g

Sugar: 5.9g
Protein: 4.9g
Cholesterol: 0mg

## INGREDIENTS

1 ¾ cup boiling water
2 cups oats (quick cooking or old-fashioned rolled)
½ cup honey
2 teaspoons salt
2 packages yeast (or 5 teaspoons yeast)
½ cup warm water
4 cups finely ground whole wheat flour, such as
    Wheat Montana

If you can't find finely ground whole wheat flour, you can use half all-purpose flour and half stone ground whole wheat flour for the best texture and taste.

## DIRECTIONS

Mix the boiling water, oats, honey, and salt in a medium bowl until the honey is dissolved. Let stand for 5 minutes. In another small bowl, whisk the yeast into the warm water until dissolved and let stand until foamy, about 5 minutes.

Measure the whole wheat flour into a large mixing bowl. Add in the honey-oat and yeast mixtures and stir vigorously with a wooden spoon to make a dough. Turn the dough onto a floured work surface. Knead for 5–8 minutes. Shape into 2 loaves and press into 2 greased loaf pans. Cover each with greased plastic wrap and let rise for 45 minutes or until doubled in size.

Preheat oven to 400°F and bake for 25–30 minutes, or until you can hear a hollow sound when you knock on the loaf. Roll the loaves out of the pans and let cool for at least 10 minutes before slicing.

## OPTIONS AND IDEAS

CINNAMON RAISIN BREAD: Add ½ cup raisins and 1 tablespoon cinnamon to the flour before mixing in the wet ingredients.

GRILLED CHEESE: Layer slices of your favorite cheese on 1 slice. Top with another slice of bread. Spread a thin layer of butter on each piece of bread and cook on a griddle or frying pan until golden on both sides.

WHOLE WHEAT BREADCRUMBS: If you happen to have any of this bread left, pulse the leftover pieces in a food processor to use as breadcrumbs for any recipe. Store in freezer in an air-tight freezer bag for up to 6 months.

# WHOLE WHEAT BANANA BREAD

I usually buy a large amount of bananas when I grocery shop because they are an inexpensive fresh fruit. Banana bread is my favorite way to use overripe bananas. Usually the loaf lasts

only a day or so because my husband eats it all. This recipe makes two loaves—one for now and one to freeze for another day!

**PREP TIME:** 15 minutes   **BAKE TIME:** 50–60 minutes
**MAKES:** 2 loaves   **SERVINGS:** 24 slices
**TOTAL COST:** $4.25

## NUTRITIONAL INFORMATION

Calories: 138

Total Fat: 2.7g

Saturated Fat: 1.4g

Sodium: 209.3mg

Carbohydrates: 27.3g

Fiber: 2.7g

Sugar: 12.6g

Protein: 3.1g

Cholesterol: 20.7mg

## INGREDIENTS

6 very ripe, large bananas

1 cup sugar

2 eggs

¼ cup plain Greek yogurt

2 teaspoons vanilla

¼ cup melted unsalted butter

3 cups finely ground whole wheat flour, such
   as Wheat Montana

2 teaspoons baking soda

1 teaspoon salt

## DIRECTIONS

Preheat oven to 325°F and grease 2 loaf pans with cooking spray. In a large bowl, mash bananas with a potato masher or sturdy fork. Add in sugar, eggs, Greek yogurt, vanilla, and melted butter, and whisk until combined. In a separate medium bowl, combine whole wheat flour, baking soda, and salt. Add the flour mixture to the banana mixture all at once and whisk until all of the flour is mixed in. The batter will be lumpy. Pour evenly into the 2 loaf pans and bake for about 50–60 minutes, or until a toothpick comes out clean when inserted into the middle of the loaf. Let cool in the pan for a few minutes and then roll out onto a cooling rack to cool completely.

> **MONEY SAVING TIP FROM LAUREN'S KITCHEN**
> If you want to freeze one loaf for later, wrap a cooled loaf completely in plastic wrap. Then wrap with heavy duty aluminum foil. This bread freezes well for up to 1 month.

# ZUCCHINI BREAD

Because of the massive harvests of squash in the summer, zucchini breads are a popular seasonal breakfast sweet bread in central Pennsylvania. Spread on a teaspoon of butter, peanut butter, or pumpkin butter, and eat it with a hot cup of tea or coffee.

**PREP TIME:** 20 minutes     **BAKE TIME:** 40–45 minutes
**MAKES:** 2 loaves     **SERVINGS:** 24 slices
*TOTAL COST:* $6.85

## NUTRITIONAL INFORMATION

| | | |
|---|---|---|
| Calories: 145 | Sodium: 167mg | Sugar: 13.5g |
| Total Fat: 3.2g | Carbohydrates: 18.7g | Protein: 3.9g |
| Saturated Fat: 0.3g | Fiber: 11.9g | Cholesterol: 15.5mg |

## INGREDIENTS

3 cups finely ground whole wheat flour, such as Wheat Montana
2 teaspoons cinnamon
½ teaspoon nutmeg
1 teaspoon baking soda

1 teaspoon salt
½ teaspoon baking powder
1 ½ cups sugar
¼ cup oil
⅓ cup plain Greek yogurt
2 eggs

2 teaspoons vanilla
2 cups shredded zucchini, seeds removed and discarded

## DIRECTIONS

Preheat oven to 350°F. Spray 2 loaf pans with cooking spray. In a medium mixing bowl, combine the whole wheat flour, cinnamon, nutmeg, baking soda, salt, and baking powder. Set aside.

> **No zucchini on hand? Try yellow squash instead!**

In another large mixing bowl, combine sugar, oil, Greek yogurt, eggs, and vanilla with an electric mixer. Add the zucchini and mix again. Add the bowl of the dry ingredients and mix just until all of the dry ingredients are incorporated. Pour the batter into the 2 loaf pans. Bake for 40–45 minutes or until a toothpick comes out clean when inserted. Let cool for 5 minutes in the pan and then remove to a rack to cool completely.

# BY-THE-BAY BISCUITS

These are some of the best biscuits you will ever taste! My students love to make these Red-Lobster-style biscuits at school—they complement almost any meal well. Use leftover biscuits (if there are any) to make Black Friday Blast Sandwiches over the holidays.

**PREP TIME:** 5 minutes
**BAKE TIME:** 8–10 minutes
**SERVINGS:** 12 biscuits
*TOTAL COST:* $2.05

## NUTRITIONAL INFORMATION

Calories: 113

Total Fat: 4.9g

Saturated Fat: 2.3g

Sodium: 275.8mg

Carbohydrates: 14.5g

Fiber: 0g

Sugar: 2.3g

Protein: 3.2g

Cholesterol: 10.8mg

## INGREDIENTS

2 cups Heart Smart Bisquick Baking Mix

½ cup cheddar cheese, shredded

¾ teaspoon garlic powder, divided

⅔ cup low-fat milk

2 tablespoons unsalted butter

¼ teaspoon Old Bay seasoning

¼ teaspoon salt

½ teaspoon dried parsley

## DIRECTIONS

Preheat oven to 425°F. Line a baking sheet with parchment paper. In a medium mixing bowl, combine the Bisquick, cheddar cheese, ½ teaspoon of garlic powder, and milk with a wooden spoon. Mix until a thick, sticky dough forms. Drop dough into 12 even–sized balls on the parchment paper with at least 2 inches between each biscuit. Bake for 8–10 minutes or until golden on the bottom.

As your biscuits bake, melt the butter in a small microwave-safe bowl. Add the remaining ¼ teaspoon of garlic powder, Old Bay seasoning, salt, and parsley to the melted butter and stir to combine. When the biscuits are finished baking, brush the butter mixture onto the top of the biscuits and serve warm.

### BLACK FRIDAY BLAST SANDWICH!

Take a biscuit and slice it in half like a burger bun. On the bottom half, layer 1–2 tablespoons cranberry sauce, leftover Thanksgiving turkey breast, and 1 slice of Gouda cheese. Broil for 30 seconds to melt cheese, top with the top half of the biscuit, and enjoy!

# EASY CHEESY GARLIC BREAD

Coming from an Italian family, I must serve garlic bread with any pasta dish or bowl of soup. This dipper pairs well with any sauce or broth and is super simple to make. You can easily double this recipe for a crowd, or else it will be gone before you even get a slice for yourself!

**TOTAL TIME:** 10 minutes
**SERVINGS:** 10 pieces
*TOTAL COST:* $3.16

**NUTRITIONAL INFORMATION** (using French baguette)

Calories: 130
Total Fat: 3.4g
Saturated Fat: 1.8g

Sodium: 355.8mg
Carbohydrates: 21.2g
Fiber: 1.1g

Sugar: 0g
Protein: 0.9g
Cholesterol: 7.8mg

## INGREDIENTS

*Bread Options*

10 slices rustic Italian, multigrain, or whole wheat French bread
1 loaf of French baguette, sliced in half lengthwise and cut into 10 total pieces
5 whole wheat sub rolls, cut in half
5 Ciabatta sandwich rolls, cut in half

*Garlic Cheese Topping*

2 tablespoons butter
¼ teaspoon garlic powder
¼ teaspoon dried basil
½ teaspoon dried parsley
½ teaspoon dried oregano
Salt and pepper to season
¼ cup parmesan cheese, grated

## DIRECTIONS

Adjust the racks in your oven so that the top rack is on the second slot from the top (about 6 inches away from the broiler). Preheat the broiler to HIGH. Line a baking sheet with foil or coat lightly with cooking spray.

Spread the butter over each piece of bread. Sprinkle each piece with garlic powder, basil, parsley, oregano, salt, and pepper. Sprinkle parmesan cheese on top. Broil the garlic toasts for 30–60 seconds or until the cheese is melted and the bread is toasted. Don't forget to set your timer—it browns very quickly! Serve with your best Italian meal or favorite soup.

# CHEESE-STUFFED BREADSTICKS
## WITH CRACKED BLACK PEPPER

My family cheered upon the introduction of the stuffed crust pizza when I was young. These breadsticks are like eating the crust of that pizza, but with cracked black pepper and a sprinkle of salt. They are simply divine. Serve with a side of marinara or with a bowl of steaming hot soup.

**PREP TIME:** 15 minutes     **RISE TIME:** 30 minutes     **BAKE TIME:** 15–17 minutes
**SERVINGS:** 8 breadsticks
**TOTAL COST:** $2.27

## NUTRITIONAL INFORMATION

Calories: 161              Sodium: 415.8mg            Sugar: 0g
Total Fat: 5.2g            Carbohydrates: 24.9g       Protein: 6.2g
Saturated Fat: 1.2g        Fiber: 4g                  Cholesterol: 4mg

## INGREDIENTS

1–2 tablespoons flour
1 pound whole wheat pizza dough, thawed (or
    make your own—see p. 84)
½ cup parmesan or sharp white cheddar
    cheese, grated

1 tablespoon olive oil
About ½ teaspoon cracked black pepper,
Salt for seasoning

## DIRECTIONS

Flour a flat counter surface with 1 tablespoon of flour. Knead the pizza dough a few times to work in the flour. Cut the dough into 8 pieces and spread each piece into a long flat rectangle. You may want to add 1 more tablespoon of flour to the counter as you complete this step if the dough is sticky. Spread 1 tablespoon of parmesan along the middle of the dough. Fold the dough over to cover the parmesan cheese and pinch to seal. Lay the stuffed breadsticks on a greased baking sheet about 1 inch apart, seam side down. Cover with a kitchen towel and let rise for 30 minutes in a warm place.

Preheat oven to 375°F. Brush the breadsticks with olive oil and top with freshly cracked black pepper and salt. Bake for 15–17 minutes or until golden brown. Serve immediately.

# WHOLE WHEAT PIZZA DOUGH

To freeze your dough, place in a quart-sized freezer bag and remove all of the excess air. Seal completely and freeze for up to 2 months. When ready to use, thaw completely in the refrigerator. Allow the thawed dough to come to room temperature before using.

Making your own pizza dough isn't hard! Taste of Home created an amazing pizza dough recipe that I just cannot top. It's simple to follow and makes enough for 3 large pizzas. I usually use one ball of dough for dinner and freeze the other two dough balls for later use.

**PREP TIME:** 15 minutes
**RISE TIME:** 20 minutes
**MAKES:** 3 pounds (enough for 3 large pizzas)
**SERVINGS:** 24 servings, 2 ounces (⅛ of 1 pound) each
*TOTAL COST:* $5.39

## NUTRITIONAL INFORMATION

Calories: 114
Total Fat: 2g
Saturated Fat: 0.5g

Sodium: 148.5mg
Carbohydrates: 21.5g
Fiber: 3.5g

Sugar: 1g
Protein: 4g
Cholesterol: 0mg

## INGREDIENTS

2 ½ cups warm water, about 105°F
3 packages or 7 ½ teaspoons of quick rise yeast
2 tablespoons sugar
5 to 6 cups finely ground whole wheat flour or white whole wheat flour, divided
1 ½ teaspoons salt
3 tablespoons olive oil

If you can't find finely ground whole wheat flour, use 3 cups stone ground whole wheat and 3 cups all-purpose flour instead.

## DIRECTIONS

In a medium bowl, whisk the warm water, yeast, and sugar until the yeast is completely dissolved. Set aside. In a large bowl, measure out 4 cups of whole wheat flour and combine it with the salt. Once the yeast is foamy and bubbly, add it to the flour mixture along with the olive oil. Mix until a dough ball forms.

Sprinkle ½ cup of the remaining flour onto a clean counter surface. Turn the dough onto the floured area and knead for 6–8 minutes. Work in additional flour from the remaining 1 ½ cups as needed, until the dough is no longer sticky. Place in the mixing bowl and cover with plastic wrap and let rise for 20 minutes. Punch down and divide into 3 pieces. Use immediately for your amazing pizza, refrigerate, or freeze for up to 2 months.

## USES FOR THIS DOUGH

- Use 1 pound of dough to make one of my pizza recipes, Pesto Prosciutto Pizza (p. 134) or Lauren K's Perfect Pizza (p. 180).
- Use 1 pound of dough for Lauren K's Sicilian Stromboli (p. 142) or your own favorite Stromboli.
- Use 1 pound of dough for Reuben Pockets with Homemade Thousand Island Dressing (p. 156).
- Use 1 pound of dough for Cheese Stuffed Breadsticks with Cracked Black Pepper (p. 83).

# SALADS & SOUPS

ASIAN CABBAGE SALAD

CHICKEN CAESAR SALAD WITH HOMEMADE CROUTONS

CURRY CHICKEN SALAD

RAINBOW CHICKPEA SALAD

CHERRY, ALMOND, AND BLUE CHEESE SALAD
WITH HONEY BALSAMIC DRESSING

BUTTERNUT SQUASH SALAD WITH CARAMELIZED ONIONS AND FETA

STRAWBERRY SPINACH SALAD WITH CREAMY POPPY SEED DRESSING

ROASTED CHICKEN AND POTATO SALAD
WITH HONEY MUSTARD DRESSING

CORN CHOWDER WITH BACON CRUMBLES AND GARLIC SHRIMP

TURKEY CORN CHILI

YELLOW POTATO, TOMATO, AND SQUASH STEW

WEEKNIGHT VEGETABLE SOUP

SUMMER GAZPACHO

CREAMY TOMATO BASIL SOUP
WITH GOUDA GRILLED CHEESE SANDWICH

LAUREN K'S "WEDDING" SOUP

# ASIAN CABBAGE SALAD

My mom makes an amazing nutty cabbage salad that everyone loves at summer picnics. I've put my own twist on her dish to lighten it up a bit without sacrificing flavor. It's a great warm weather side because it doesn't need to be chilled and can be made in advance—just add the dressing and toss right before your event. You could even top leftovers with cooked chicken breast for lunch the next day.

**TOTAL TIME:** 15 minutes
**SERVINGS:** 10, about 1 cup each
*TOTAL COST:* $5.58

### NUTRITIONAL INFORMATION

| | | |
|---|---|---|
| Calories: 191 | Sodium: 230mg | Sugar: 2.7g |
| Total Fat: 14g | Carbohydrates: 14.6g | Protein: 3.7g |
| Saturated Fat: 2.3g | Fiber: 3g | Cholesterol: 0mg |

### INGREDIENTS

**Salad**
1 medium head cabbage, shredded (about 2 pounds or 10 cups)
½ cup slivered or sliced almonds
3 tablespoons toasted sesame seeds
1 package oriental flavored ramen noodles, dry noodles broken and seasoning packet reserved

**Dressing**
¼ cup extra virgin olive oil
2 tablespoons sesame oil
3 tablespoons white or apple cider vinegar
2 tablespoons sugar
½ teaspoon salt
¼ teaspoon pepper

- If you can't find toasted sesame seeds, you can toast them yourself in a skillet over medium-low heat. Keep an eye on them as they brown easily.

- Sesame oil adds a nutty flavor, but you can replace it with olive oil if needed.

## DIRECTIONS

**SALAD:** Place shredded cabbage in a large serving bowl. Next, toast the almonds in a skillet over medium-low heat. Turn them with a spatula frequently, as they will burn quickly. Once they are lightly browned, add the toasted almonds, toasted sesame seeds, and crushed ramen noodles to shredded cabbage.

**DRESSING:** In a separate small bowl, combine the ramen noodle seasoning packet, olive oil, sesame oil, vinegar, sugar, salt, and pepper. Whisk until thoroughly combined. If making ahead of time, store dressing in a container. Before serving, add the dressing to the cabbage mix and toss to combine.

## FUN FACT

This recipe contains 47% of your daily requirement of Vitamin C. Surprisingly, cabbage is a great source of this infection-fighting vitamin. Eat up and keep those sniffles away!

# CHICKEN CAESAR SALAD
## *WITH HOMEMADE CROUTONS*

Homemade dressings and fun salad toppers turn my lunch salad into something I look forward to all morning. This recipe features homemade croutons, lean chicken breast, and a homemade Caesar dressing that will make your lunch buddies jealous!

**BAKE TIME:** 20–25 minutes    **TOTAL TIME:** 35 minutes

**SERVINGS:** 4 entrée salads

**TOTAL COST:** $9.95

## NUTRITIONAL INFORMATION

Calories: 443

Total Fat: 24.1g

Saturated Fat: 5.1g

Sodium: 767.7mg

Carbohydrates: 20.3g

Fiber: 2.6g

Sugar: 1g

Protein: 35.6g

Cholesterol: 91.9mg

## INGREDIENTS

**Salad**

1 pound boneless skinless chicken breasts

4 thick slices day-old hearty bread (rustic Italian, multigrain, whole wheat
    French loaf or baguette)

1 tablespoon extra virgin olive oil

2 heads romaine lettuce, roughly chopped (about 8 cups)

½ cup freshly grated parmesan cheese

**Dressing**

Juice of 1 lemon

1 tablespoon Dijon mustard

1 clove garlic, minced and smashed into a paste with
    the back of your knife

1 tablespoon anchovy paste (optional)

4 tablespoons extra virgin olive oil

Salt and freshly ground black pepper, to taste

> Depending on the grocer, you can find anchovy paste near the canned anchovies and sardines or with the tomato paste.

## DIRECTIONS

**SALAD:** Preheat oven to 350°F. Line a rimmed baking sheet with foil and coat with cooking spray. Lay out chicken breasts and season with salt and pepper on both sides. Bake for about 20–25 minutes or until the chicken is no longer pink in the middle. Let rest for 5 minutes and slice into strips for the salad.

For the croutons, cube the bread into 1-inch cubes. Drizzle with 1 tablespoon of olive oil and season with salt and pepper. Toss to coat. Toast bread cubes in a medium skillet until toasted and browned, tossing every minute or so. The longer you toast them, the crunchier they will be.

For salad assembly, place romaine in a large bowl. Toss with the Caesar dressing to coat completely. Sprinkle half of the parmesan cheese over the romaine and toss again. Load the dressed romaine onto plates for serving and top each plate with 1 more tablespoon of parmesan cheese, a quarter of the sliced chicken, and a quarter of the croutons.

### CAESAR DRESSING:

In a small bowl, combine the lemon juice, Dijon mustard, garlic clove, and anchovy paste with a small whisk. Whisk in 4 tablespoons olive oil until completely combined. Season dressing with salt and pepper to taste.

**PLAN AHEAD!**
Double the dressing recipe and save half in a sealed jar in the refrigerator. Store for up to 1 week.

# CURRY CHICKEN SALAD

Sunday is my big day to make lunches for the week. This one's a staple in my house. It pairs well with any bread, ranging from pitas to English muffins, and it tastes wonderful on its own!

**BAKE TIME:** 20–25 minutes    **TOTAL TIME:** 30 minutes
**SERVINGS:** 8, 1 cup each
*TOTAL COST:* $10.09

## NUTRITIONAL INFORMATION

Calories: 222

Total Fat: 7.8g

Saturated Fat: 1.3g

Sodium: 334.7mg

Carbohydrates: 11.6g

Fiber: 1.7g

Sugar: 8.2g

Protein: 26g

Cholesterol: 70.2mg

## INGREDIENTS

2 pounds boneless skinless chicken breast

Salt and pepper to season

2 cups apples, diced

1 cup celery, diced

½ cup sweetened dried cranberries, roughly chopped

½ cup light mayonnaise

1 tablespoon yellow curry powder

¼ cup water

½ teaspoon salt

¼ teaspoon freshly grated black pepper

## DIRECTIONS

Preheat oven to 350°F. Line a rimmed baking sheet with foil and coat with cooking spray. Lay out chicken breasts and season with salt and pepper on both sides. Bake for about 20–25 minutes or until the chicken is no longer pink in the middle. Let cool and then cut into small cubes.

Combine cubed chicken breast, diced apples, diced celery, and chopped dried cranberries in a large bowl. In a separate small mixing bowl, combine the mayonnaise, yellow curry powder, water, salt, and pepper. Whisk these ingredients together until well blended. Pour the dressing over the chicken mixture and toss to coat evenly. Serve with your favorite bread or over a salad of mixed greens.

# RAINBOW CHICKPEA SALAD

Every college student knows how hard it is to eat healthy with little money to spend. My roommate Erin and I were adamant about eating well but sticking to our budget, so this salad was on the menu week after week! It works well as a meatless main dish for two or as a four-serving side dish to accompany your favorite protein. This was actually one of my very first recipes I ever created on my own, and I still use it today!

**TOTAL TIME:** 5 minutes
**SERVINGS:** 2 main dishes (2 heaping cups each) or 4 side dishes (1 heaping cup each)
*TOTAL COST:* $4.38

**NUTRITIONAL INFORMATION** (main dish serving)

| | | |
|---|---|---|
| Calories: 395 | Sodium: 931.7mg | Sugar: 11.5g |
| Total Fat: 10.9g | Carbohydrates: 68.5g | Protein: 17g |
| Saturated Fat: 1.2g | Fiber: 14.5g | Cholesterol: 0mg |

## INGREDIENTS

1 cup fresh or frozen corn, thawed
1 cup frozen peas, thawed
1 pint cherry or grape tomatoes, halved, OR 2 cups fresh tomatoes, diced
15-ounce can chickpeas/garbanzo beans, drained and rinsed
1 tablespoon extra virgin olive oil
3 tablespoons red wine vinegar
Salt and pepper to season (about ¼ teaspoon each)

## DIRECTIONS

Combine the corn, peas, cherry tomato halves, and chickpeas in a medium serving bowl. Drizzle the extra virgin olive oil and red wine vinegar over the mixture. Season with salt and pepper, toss to coat, and serve.

# CHERRY, ALMOND, AND BLUE CHEESE SALAD
## WITH HONEY BALSAMIC DRESSING

Fresh cherries are the candy of nature! Most people save cherries for pies and desserts, but this fruit also makes amazing salads and savory dishes. This salad is so refreshing in the summertime when cherries are in their peak season. The mixture of smoky almonds, salty blue cheese, and sweet cherries make this salad one of my summer favorites. Enjoy!

**TOTAL TIME:** 20 minutes
**SERVINGS:** 5, about 1 ⅓ cups each
*TOTAL COST:* $8.24

### NUTRITIONAL INFORMATION

| | | |
|---|---|---|
| Calories: 267 | Sodium: 281.3mg | Sugar: 12.1g |
| Total Fat: 19.5g | Carbohydrates: 18.4g | Protein: 8.2g |
| Saturated Fat: 3.7g | Fiber: 4.2g | Cholesterol: 8.5mg |

### INGREDIENTS

**Salad**
1 cup slivered almonds
1 ½ romaine hearts, washed and chopped (about 5 cups)
½ pound cherries, pitted and quartered (about 20 large cherries)
½ cup blue cheese or gorgonzola, crumbled

**Dressing**
2 tablespoons extra virgin olive oil
2 tablespoons balsamic vinegar
2 tablespoons honey
¼ teaspoon salt
¼ teaspoon pepper

> **When cherries are out of season, substitute sliced pears or golden delicious apples.**

### DIRECTIONS

**SALAD:** In a medium skillet, toast the slivered almonds over medium-low heat, stirring frequently to prevent burning. Place romaine in a large serving bowl and toss with the dressing. Top the salad with cherries, toasted almonds, and blue cheese crumbles. Serve cold or at room temperature.

**DRESSING:** In a small bowl, whisk together the extra virgin olive oil, balsamic vinegar, honey, salt, and pepper.

# BUTTERNUT SQUASH SALAD
## WITH CARAMELIZED ONIONS AND FETA

I made this recipe during a demonstration to my students about how you can turn leftover ingredients into a new dish. The combination of these summer harvest flavors and balsamic vinegar tastes wonderful.

**TOTAL TIME:** 35 minutes
**SERVINGS:** 6, 1 cup each
*TOTAL COST:* $10.41

### NUTRITIONAL INFORMATION

| | | |
|---|---|---|
| Calories: 189.6 | Sodium: 299.8mg | Sugar: 2.7g |
| Total Fat: 8.8g | Carbohydrates: 24.5g | Protein: 5g |
| Saturated Fat: 3.4g | Fiber: 6.3g | Cholesterol: 16.8mg |

### INGREDIENTS

1 medium butternut squash, about 3 pounds, peeled and cut into 1-inch cubes (about 5–6 cups)

2 tablespoons olive oil, divided

Salt and pepper to season

2 medium onions, sliced (about 3 cups)

1 tablespoon plus ¼ cup balsamic vinegar, divided

1 teaspoon sugar

4 cups mixed greens

⅓ cup parsley, chopped

4 ounces feta cheese, crumbled

### DIRECTIONS

Preheat oven to 400°F. Lay the cubed butternut squash on a large rimmed baking sheet lined with foil, toss with 1 tablespoon olive oil, and season with salt and pepper. Roast 20 minutes or until a fork pierces the squash cubes easily. Remove the squash from the oven and let cool for 5 minutes.

While the squash bakes, in a large skillet, combine sliced onions, 1 tablespoon of balsamic vinegar, 1 tablespoon olive oil, and 1 teaspoon sugar. Cook over medium-low heat and stir occasionally for about 30 minutes or until onions are browned and caramelized. If you begin to see black charring, turn down the heat. Allow the onions to cool for 5 minutes.

In a large serving bowl, combine the squash cubes, mixed greens, caramelized onions, parsley, and feta crumbles. Drizzle the mixture with ¼ cup balsamic vinegar. Toss to coat and serve.

# STRAWBERRY SPINACH SALAD
## *WITH CREAMY POPPY SEED DRESSING*

Sweet, refreshing salads are the perfect summertime lunch. Sweet strawberries, candied pecans, and spinach pair very well with this creamy, homemade dressing. Add grilled chicken or salmon on top for a complete meal.

**TOTAL TIME:** 10 minutes
**SERVINGS:** 4 lunch portions
*TOTAL COST:* $8.42

### NUTRITIONAL INFORMATION

Calories: 211

Total Fat: 11.1g

Saturated Fat: 1.2g

Sodium: 238.9mg

Carbohydrates: 25.2g

Fiber: 4.3g

Sugar: 20.1g

Protein: 4.8g

Cholesterol: 0mg

### INGREDIENTS

**Salad**

1 pint strawberries, cleaned and sliced

10 ounces fresh spinach

½ cup candied or glazed pecans or walnuts
   (See Spiced Pecans, p. 224, to make them yourself)

**Dressing**

¼ cup light mayonnaise

2 tablespoons plain Greek yogurt

1 tablespoon poppy seeds

3 tablespoons sugar

2 tablespoons red wine vinegar

Salt and pepper to season

## DIRECTIONS

**SALAD:** Place spinach and strawberries in a large serving bowl. Pour dressing over the spinach salad and toss to coat. Top with candied pecans and serve immediately.

**DRESSING:** In a sealable jar, add the light mayonnaise, Greek yogurt, poppy seeds, sugar, and red wine vinegar. Season with salt and pepper. Shake vigorously for about 30 seconds to combine all ingredients.

## MAKE-AHEAD LUNCH IDEA

Layer the spinach, strawberries and pecans into 4 large to-go containers. Distribute the dressing evenly among 4 small separate containers. Put the dressing container inside the salad container, and you have 4 on-the-go lunches ready in a flash! Keep refrigerated until serving.

# ROASTED CHICKEN AND POTATO SALAD
## WITH HONEY MUSTARD DRESSING

I love to mix and match veggies and dressings into my salads. This lunch or dinner dish features roasted potatoes and chicken breast, both affordable ingredients at any grocery store. Chicken is my preferred protein for salad, but feel free to use your own favorite. Make extra roasted potatoes and save them to make a Farmhouse Crustless Quiche!

**PREP TIME:** 25 minutes   **BAKE TIME:** 30 minutes
**SERVINGS:** 4 entrée salads
**TOTAL COST:** $13.95

### NUTRITIONAL INFORMATION

Calories: 510
Total Fat: 17.7g
Saturated Fat: 2.8g

Sodium: 549.8mg
Carbohydrates: 58.6g
Fiber: 5.5g

Sugar: 21g
Protein: 33g
Cholesterol: 70.2mg

### INGREDIENTS

**Salad**
3 cups yellow potatoes, cut into 1-inch cubes
2 tablespoons olive oil, divided
Salt and pepper to season
1 pound boneless skinless chicken breast
4 medium slices hearty Italian or French
    bread, about ½-inch thick
2 heads romaine lettuce
2 medium tomatoes
1 large cucumber, peeled

**Dressing**
¼ cup honey
¼ cup Dijon mustard
2 tablespoons olive oil
Salt and pepper to season

## DIRECTIONS

**SALAD:** Preheat oven to 375°F. Line 2 large rimmed baking sheets with foil. Lay cubed potatoes in an even layer on 1 baking sheet. Drizzle with 1 tablespoon of olive oil and season with salt and pepper. Toss to coat. Roast potatoes in the oven for 30 minutes. Meanwhile, cut larger chicken breasts in half if needed so there are 4 thin breasts total. Season each side with salt and pepper. When the potatoes have 20 minutes left, remove the baking sheet from the oven. Push the potatoes to one side, still keeping them in an even layer. Place seasoned chicken breasts on the other side of the pan and place back into the oven.

As the chicken and potatoes roast, cube the Italian bread slices into 1-inch crouton-sized cubes. Drizzle with 1 tablespoon of olive oil, season with salt and pepper, and toss to coat with your hands. Lay the croutons out on the second baking sheet in an even layer. When the potatoes and chicken have 10 minutes left, add the croutons to the other rack in your oven. The chicken, potatoes, and croutons will all be done at the same time. Be sure that the chicken is cooked all the way through, with no pink inside.

Meanwhile, cut up the romaine, tomatoes, and cucumbers and place them in a large serving bowl. Drizzle dressing evenly over vegetables and toss to coat. When the chicken, potatoes, and croutons are done baking, remove from the oven and let cool for 5 minutes. Slice the chicken and top the salad with potatoes, chicken, and croutons.

**DRESSING:** In a small bowl, combine the honey, Dijon mustard, and 2 tablespoons of olive oil with a whisk. Season with salt and pepper and whisk again until the dressing is thoroughly combined.

## FARMHOUSE CRUSTLESS QUICHE

Cube an additional 2 cups of potatoes to roast with the potatoes from this recipe (also add an additional ½ tablespoon olive oil). Use the Broccoli and Feta Crustless Quiche recipe on p. 54, but replace the broccoli with roasted potatoes and substitute cheddar cheese for feta. This makes a quick morning breakfast!

# CORN CHOWDER
## WITH BACON CRUMBLES AND GARLIC SHRIMP

Many soups I've had at restaurants taste delicious, but do not sit well in my stomach afterwards because of all of the cream and butter. I've come up a velvety corn chowder for under $2.07 per serving that doesn't need all of those unhealthy ingredients to be a star dish. With a little bacon for flavor and juicy garlic shrimp on top, you'll be grabbing a straw to slurp up the last few drops!

**TOTAL TIME:** 35 minutes
**SERVINGS:** 8, each with 1 ¾ cups soup, 2 ounces shrimp, 1 tablespoon green onions, and
    1 tablespoon bacon crumbles
*TOTAL COST:* $16.63

### NUTRITIONAL INFORMATION

| | | |
|---|---|---|
| Calories: 264 | Sodium: 751.3mg | Sugar: 6.6g |
| Total Fat: 9.9g | Carbohydrates: 26.3g | Protein: 19.7g |
| Saturated Fat: 2.8g | Fiber: 3.4g | Cholesterol: 97.9mg |

### INGREDIENTS

5 slices thick-cut bacon, roughly chopped
2 tablespoons olive oil, divided
6 cloves garlic, minced and divided
1 pound raw shrimp, peeled, deveined, and
    tails removed
Salt and pepper to season

1 large onion, chopped
32 ounces chicken broth
5 cups fresh or frozen corn kernels
1 teaspoon paprika
2 cups low-fat milk
½ cup green onions, chopped

> Swap the shrimp for crab to make Crab Corn Chowder!

## DIRECTIONS

In a large skillet, cook the bacon until crispy. Remove to a plate lined with paper towels to absorb the excess fat. Once it is cool enough to touch, crumble the bacon. Pour out the bacon fat into a sturdy container for cooling and then discard. Wipe out the pan with a paper towel, heat over medium heat, and add 1 tablespoon of olive oil. Sauté half of the garlic for 30 seconds. Add the shrimp and season the mixture with salt and pepper. Stir to coat and sauté for 3–4 minutes, stirring occasionally. Cook just until the shrimp is completely pink. Do not overcook. Remove from the pan and place on a plate while you make your soup. Cover with foil to keep hot.

In a large soup pot or Dutch oven, add the remaining 1 tablespoon of olive oil, onions, and remaining garlic to the pan. Cook over medium heat for 4–5 minutes until the onions are translucent, stirring occasionally. Add chicken broth, corn, and paprika, and season with salt and pepper. Bring to a boil and remove from heat. Pour 4 cups of soup into a blender, and blend until smooth. Pour back into the pan, add the milk, and stir to combine. Cook over medium heat just until simmering. Do not boil. Ladle into bowls and top with shrimp, crumbled bacon, and green onions. Serve hot with a piece of crusty whole wheat bread for dipping.

## FREEZER TIP

This recipe makes *a lot* of soup. If you have leftovers that you don't want to eat right away, ladle your soup into freezer bags or thick plastic containers. Seal tightly and freeze for up to 3 months. To thaw, place in the refrigerator the night before eating. Reheat in a saucepan and serve.

# TURKEY CORN CHILI

Who doesn't love to come home to a warm bowl of chili on a cold day? This chili features lean turkey with a combination of protein-packed beans and veggies to warm your soul. Serve with a slice of Easy Cheesy Garlic Bread (p. 82), Honey Oatmeal Bread (p. 76), or your favorite cornbread for a complete meal.

**TOTAL TIME:** 35 minutes
**SERVINGS:** 12, about 1 ½ cups each
*TOTAL COST:* $13.21*

**NUTRITIONAL INFORMATION***

| | | |
|---|---|---|
| Calories: 211 | Sodium: 896.5mg | Sugar: 4g |
| Total Fat: 5g | Carbohydrates: 28.7g | Protein: 14.2g |
| Saturated Fat: 1.1g | Fiber: 7.6g | Cholesterol: 26.7mg |

*Price and nutrition do not include optional toppers.*

---

**INGREDIENTS**

1 tablespoon olive oil
1 large onion, diced
3 garlic cloves, minced
1 pound ground lean turkey breast
1 packet (1.25 ounces) low-sodium chili seasoning, such as McCormick's
28 ounces tomato sauce
1 15-ounce can mild chili beans

2 15-ounce cans dark or light kidney beans, drained and rinsed
1 15-ounce can Great Northern beans, drained and rinsed
2 cups frozen or fresh corn kernels

*Optional Toppers:* sour cream, cheddar cheese, green onions, or crackers*

---

**DIRECTIONS**

Heat a large Dutch oven over medium heat. Add olive oil, onions, and garlic, and sauté until onions are translucent, about 4–5 minutes. Add ground turkey and stir it in, breaking into small pieces, until browned. Sprinkle chili seasoning mix over the browned turkey and stir to combine. Let the mixture cook for 1 more minute.

Add the tomato sauce, mild chili beans, kidney beans, and Great Northern beans into the turkey mixture. Stir until combined. Bring the mixture to a simmer and then reduce heat to low. Simmer the chili, stirring every 5 minutes, for 15–20 minutes. Add the corn kernels right before serving.

# YELLOW POTATO, TOMATO, AND SQUASH STEW

My husband's uncle, David Kudlawiec, has quite a green thumb and grows amazing yellow squash. He brings me bags of them during the summer to see what dishes I can create. This is one of those "throw in the kitchen sink while you're at it" late-summer recipes. It has just the right amount of spice, and it's packed full of veggies that will leave your stomach satisfied.

**TOTAL TIME:** 40 minutes
**SERVINGS:** 5, 2 cups each
*TOTAL COST:* $12.77

### NUTRITIONAL INFORMATION

Calories: 185
Total Fat: 3.4g
Saturated Fat: 0.5g

Sodium: 807.6mg
Carbohydrates: 35g
Fiber: 6.7g

Sugar: 3.3g
Protein: 6g
Cholesterol: 4mg

### INGREDIENTS

1 tablespoon olive oil
2 medium onions, chopped
3–4 cloves garlic, minced
1 bay leaf
4 cups Yukon gold potatoes, cut into 1-inch cubes
Salt and pepper to season
1 tablespoon fresh thyme, chopped, or 1 teaspoon dried

1 tablespoon fresh dill, chopped, or 1 teaspoon dried
4 cups shredded yellow squash, zucchini, or cooked spaghetti squash
1 teaspoon curry powder
1 teaspoon paprika, preferably smoked or Hungarian
4 cups 99% fat free chicken or vegetable broth
2 cups tomatoes, diced
2 tablespoons fresh parsley, chopped

### DIRECTIONS

Heat 1 tablespoon of olive oil in a Dutch oven or large stock pot over medium heat. Add the onions, garlic, and bay leaf and sauté for 3 minutes. Add the potatoes and season with salt and pepper. Sauté the mixture for 4–5 minutes, stirring occasionally. Add thyme, dill, squash, curry powder, and paprika. Stir to combine and sauté for 2 more minutes. Add the chicken or vegetable broth and bring to a simmer. Simmer for about 8 minutes or until the potatoes break with a fork. Use a potato masher to mash the potatoes about 10 times, breaking up some of the bigger chunks. Remove from heat and stir in the tomatoes and parsley. Serve hot.

# WEEKNIGHT VEGETABLE SOUP

My mother's vegetable soup always warmed up my fingers and toes when I came in from playing in the snow with my brother and sister. The biggest highlight to this vegetable soup is that you can use any vegetables you have on hand. If you don't have corn, use green beans instead!

**TOTAL TIME:** 35 minutes
**SERVINGS:** 10, 1 cup each
*TOTAL COST:* $9.95

## NUTRITIONAL INFORMATION

Calories: 98
Total Fat: 1.8g
Saturated Fat: 0.3g

Sodium: 806.7mg
Carbohydrates: 13.9g
Fiber: 2.2g

Sugar: 3.6g
Protein: 2.3g
Cholesterol: 3mg

## INGREDIENTS

1 tablespoon olive oil
1 ½ cups onions, chopped (about 2 medium)
4 cloves garlic, minced
1 ½ cups carrots, chopped
1 ½ cups celery, chopped (about 3 stalks)
1 bay leaf

½ teaspoon salt
½ teaspoon pepper
5 cups shredded cabbage, about ½ a large head
2 14.5-ounce cans diced tomatoes
48 ounces low-fat chicken or vegetable broth
2 cups fresh or frozen corn

## DIRECTIONS

Heat 1 tablespoon olive oil in a large Dutch oven or stock pot. Add onions, garlic, carrots, celery, and bay leaf. Season with salt and pepper. Cook over medium heat until the vegetables are softened, about 8 minutes, stirring occasionally to prevent burning. Add cabbage, diced tomatoes, and chicken or vegetable broth. Bring mixture to a boil and simmer for 5 additional minutes to cook the cabbage. Stir in corn, cook for 2 minutes longer, and serve.

## STIR-IT-IN FOR UNDER 100 CALORIES

- 3 tablespoons parmesan cheese
- ⅓ cup cooked chicken or turkey breast
- ⅓ cup white beans, such as cannellini
- ¼ cup cooked brown rice
- 2 tablespoons feta cheese

# SUMMER GAZPACHO

One summer, my mom and dad had an abundance of tomatoes in their garden and were looking for new dishes to try. They used a variety of garden vegetables to make a refreshing cold soup. This soup tastes best in the summer months when tomatoes are in season. Garnish with feta cheese, fresh corn kernels, or a nice chunk of crusty multigrain bread.

**TOTAL TIME:** 20 minutes
**SERVINGS:** 8, 1 cup each
**TOTAL COST:** $8.16

## NUTRITIONAL INFORMATION

Calories: 68               Sodium: 158.3mg          Sugar: 1.3g
Total Fat: 3.9g            Carbohydrates: 8.4g      Protein: 1.6g
Saturated Fat: 0.5g       Fiber: 2.1g              Cholesterol: 0mg

## INGREDIENTS

5 large tomatoes, cubed
2 medium cucumbers, peeled, seeds removed, and diced
1 green pepper, stem and seeds removed and diced
½ cup green onions
2–3 cloves garlic

2 tablespoons fresh parsley
Juice of ½ lime
2 tablespoons olive oil
2 tablespoons red wine vinegar
½ teaspoon salt
¼ teaspoon freshly ground black pepper

## DIRECTIONS

Add all ingredients to a large food processor. Pulse 5 times and then run for 10 seconds. Serve with your favorite garnishes.

# CREAMY TOMATO BASIL SOUP
## WITH GOUDA GRILLED CHEESE SANDWICH

Here's a sad, factual story about my early days in the kitchen. When my husband Bryan (then boyfriend) came over to my parents' house one summer day, I attempted to make him lunch. I opened a can of Campbell's tomato soup and started to make some grilled cheeses. I must have been distracted by the jokes from the attractive football player in my kitchen because, before I knew it, the tomato soup had developed a nasty skin and was burned all over the bottom of the pan. It was unsalvageable. Luckily, the grilled cheeses survived. For quite some time, Bryan was the unofficial cook of our relationship. Luckily, I overcame that experience and managed to make real tomato soup from scratch!

**TOTAL TIME:** 30 minutes
**SERVINGS:** 6, 1 cup of soup and ½ sandwich each
*TOTAL COST:* $11.08

### NUTRITIONAL INFORMATION for 1 cup of soup

| | | |
|---|---|---|
| Calories: 130 | Sodium: 450mg | Sugar: 0.9g |
| Total Fat: 8.7g | Carbohydrates: 9.8g | Protein: 4.4g |
| Saturated Fat: 3.1g | Fiber: 2g | Cholesterol: 13.2mg |

### NUTRITIONAL INFORMATION for ½ grilled cheese sandwich

| | | |
|---|---|---|
| Calories: 221 | Sodium: 375.3mg | Sugar: 2.4g |
| Total Fat: 10.5g | Carbohydrates: 22.4g | Protein: 8.8g |
| Saturated Fat: 6.2g | Fiber: 1g | Cholesterol: 31.9mg |

 *Sandwich*

## INGREDIENTS

*Tomato Basil Soup*

2 tablespoons olive oil

1 medium onion, chopped

2–3 cloves garlic, minced

4 cups chopped fresh tomatoes OR 30 ounces of no-salt-added diced tomatoes

½ cup fresh basil, chopped and divided

1 ½ cups chicken or vegetable broth

Salt and pepper to season

½ cup half and half

6 tablespoons parmesan cheese, grated

*Gouda Grilled Cheese*

6 teaspoons butter

6 slices thick bakery-style sourdough bread (about 120 calories per slice)

4 ounces sliced or 1 cup grated smoked Gouda cheese (cheddar works great as a substitute)

## DIRECTIONS

**TOMATO BASIL SOUP:** In a large soup pot or Dutch oven, heat 2 tablespoons olive oil over medium heat. Add onions and garlic and sauté for about 3 minutes to soften onions. Add the tomatoes and ¼ cup basil and cook for 2 more minutes. Add the chicken or vegetable broth and season with salt and pepper. Bring to a boil and simmer for 5 minutes. Pour soup into a blender and place lid on. Wrap a kitchen towel around the entire top of the blender to prevent spattering. Blend for 10–15 seconds until the mixture is pureed. Add back into the pot and stir in half and half. Bring to a simmer and turn off heat. Do not boil. Stir in remaining chopped basil. Ladle soup into serving bowls and top with 1 tablespoon parmesan cheese per serving.

**GOUDA GRILLED CHEESE:** As you wait for your soup to simmer, prepare your grilled cheeses. Preheat a griddle or flat large skillet to medium-low heat. Spread 1 teaspoon of butter onto one side of each slice of bread. Divide the Gouda evenly among 3 slices of the bread and then top with the remaining slices of bread, butter side outward. Lay the sandwiches onto the griddle and cook for about 2–4 minutes per side until golden brown. Use a spatula to check underneath to prevent burning. Cut sandwiches in half and serve 1 sandwich half with 1 cup of soup.

# LAUREN K'S "WEDDING" SOUP

I used to make this soup for my husband in our small apartment right after we were married; he was finicky about eating vegetables, so I had to figure out creative ways to sneak them into our evening meals. The flavors remind us of homemade wedding soup, but without the effort of making dozens of mini meatballs.

**TOTAL TIME:** 25 minutes
**SERVINGS:** 10, 1 cup each
*TOTAL COST:* $10.44

## NUTRITIONAL INFORMATION

Calories: 177

Total Fat: 6.7g

Saturated Fat: 1.5g

Sodium: 1,053mg

Carbohydrates: 15.3g

Fiber: 4.8g

Sugar: 0.1g

Protein: 14.6g

Cholesterol: 33mg

## INGREDIENTS

1 tablespoon olive oil

3 cloves garlic, minced

1 large onion, chopped

1 pound turkey sausage

2 15-ounce cans Great Northern or cannellini beans, drained and rinsed

48 ounces 99% fat free chicken broth

10-ounce package frozen chopped spinach, thawed

Feel free to substitute 2 cups of cooked short-cut pasta, such as orzo, for beans.

## DIRECTIONS

Heat olive oil in a Dutch oven or stock pot over medium heat. Add minced garlic and chopped onions and cook until onions begin to soften, about 4 minutes. Crumble in raw turkey sausage and break into bite-sized pieces with a wooden spoon. When sausage is browned and cooked through, add chicken broth. Bring to a boil and then turn down to a simmer. Squeeze out all of the water from the spinach and add spinach and beans to the pot. Bring to a simmer for 2 additional minutes and serve hot.

**Sprinkle your soup with 1 tablespoon of grated parmesan cheese for only 25 additional calories.**

# POULTRY, PORK, & BEEF ENTREES

GRILLED HAWAIIAN CHICKEN KABOBS

QUICK CHICKEN STIR FRY
*WITH BROCCOLI AND SNOW PEAS*

APPLE CHEDDAR CHICKEN MEATBALLS
*WITH BROCCOLI BACON SALAD*

OVEN BAKED CHICKEN WINGS
*BUFFALO HOT WINGS, OLD BAY WINGS, GARLIC PARMESAN WINGS*

ITALIAN CHICKEN CUTLETS

BUFFALO GARLIC CROCK-POT CHICKEN

RED HOT AND BLUE SANDWICHES
*WITH CARAMELIZED ONIONS*

CHEDDAR CHICKEN TACOS

ITALIAN CHICKEN ROLL-UPS
*WITH CHRISTMAS PASTA*

CROCK-POT PULLED PORK BBQ SANDWICHES

CROCK-POT PORK AND SAUERKRAUT

APPLE CIDER PORK CHOPS *WITH APPLES AND ONIONS*

PESTO PROSCIUTTO PIZZA

GRILLED TURKEY KIELBASA
*WITH CHARRED BELL PEPPERS*

SPAGHETTI SQUASH CARBONARA

CURRY TURKEY STUFFED PEPPERS

LIGHTENED-UP LASAGNA

LAUREN K'S SICILIAN STROMBOLI

MINI PEPPER PIZZAS

ZUCCHINI PIZZAS

HARVEST STUFFED ACORN SQUASH

"SPAGHETTI" AND MEATBALLS

BEEF "GYROS" *WITH GREEK SALAD*

ITALIAN PAISAN BURGERS

MOM AND DAD'S LONDON BROIL *WITH ROASTED GARLIC GREEN BEANS*

REUBEN POCKETS
*WITH HOMEMADE THOUSAND ISLAND DRESSING*

# GRILLED HAWAIIAN CHICKEN KABOBS

When I vacationed with my husband's family in Hawaii, we tasted the most delicious pineapple on earth. This dish, with my homemade Sweet Garlic BBQ Sauce, really takes me back to the beaches of Maui.

**TOTAL TIME:** 35 minutes
**SERVINGS:** 4, about 2 kabobs each
*TOTAL COST:* $12.97

## NUTRITIONAL INFORMATION

| | | |
|---|---|---|
| Calories: 370 | Sodium: 399mg | Sugar: 45g |
| Total Fat: 2.9g | Carbohydrates: 50.3g | Protein: 41.1g |
| Saturated Fat: 0.6g | Fiber: 2.9g | Cholesterol: 112.5mg |

## INGREDIENTS

1 ½ pounds boneless skinless chicken breast, cut into 1-inch cubes

Salt and pepper to season

¾ cup Sweet Garlic BBQ Sauce (see p. 237) or your favorite BBQ sauce

1 large pineapple, cut into 1-inch cubes

8–10 wooden or metal kabob skewers

> Skewer on tomatoes, onions, or peppers to add some veggies!

## DIRECTIONS

Heat your grill to medium heat. Season chicken cubes with salt and pepper and toss with ¼ cup BBQ sauce to marinade while you cut up your pineapple. Place the pineapple in a separate bowl for easy skewering. Skewer the marinated chicken cubes alternately with the pineapple. Leave some room between each item on the skewer to allow for even cooking. Once all of the kabobs are ready, place them on the grill. Grill about 4–5 minutes on each side, basting with the remaining ½ cup sauce as they cook. Remove kabobs to a clean platter and serve.

# QUICK CHICKEN STIR FRY
## WITH BROCCOLI AND SNOW PEAS

I came up with this 12-minute meal on a snowy day when school was cancelled and I had a bunch of leftover roasted turkey. This recipe is *so* easy—a caveman could do it! Lots of veggies, lean protein, and brown rice make this a flavorful and healthy choice.

**TOTAL TIME:** 12 minutes
**SERVINGS:** 4, each about 1 ½ cups of stir fry and 1 cup of cooked rice
*TOTAL COST:* $10.26

### NUTRITIONAL INFORMATION

| | | |
|---|---|---|
| Calories: 381 | Sodium: 829mg | Sugar: 2.3g |
| Total Fat: 8g | Carbohydrates: 44.4g | Protein: 35.9g |
| Saturated Fat: 1.3g | Fiber: 7.5g | Cholesterol: 70.2mg |

### INGREDIENTS

2 cups uncooked instant brown rice

Olive oil cooking spray

1 medium head broccoli, cut into florets (about 6 cups)

Salt and pepper to season

1 tablespoon olive oil

8 ounces snow peas

1 pound cooked and shredded turkey or chicken (about 2 cups)

3 tablespoons low-sodium soy sauce

2 tablespoons hot sauce

### DIRECTIONS

Follow the package directions to cook the brown rice in a large saucepan. Allow it to cook as you make your stir fry.

Heat a large skillet over medium heat. Coat the pan with olive oil cooking spray. Add the broccoli, spray it with a little more cooking spray, and add salt and pepper. Sauté the broccoli for about 5 minutes and remove from pan.

In the same skillet, add the 1 tablespoon of olive oil and snow peas and sauté for about 3 minutes. Add turkey or chicken and heat through, about 2 more minutes. Add the broccoli back to the pan, drizzle in soy sauce and hot sauce, and toss to mix. Heat for another 2 minutes and serve with rice.

# APPLE CHEDDAR CHICKEN MEATBALLS
## *WITH BROCCOLI BACON SALAD*

This dish is a great any-time-of-the-year meal because these ingredients are usually affordable year-round.

**TOTAL TIME:** 35 minutes
**SERVINGS:** 4, each with 4 meatballs and 1 cup of salad
*TOTAL COST:* $12.10

## NUTRITIONAL INFORMATION

Calories: 467

Total Fat: 29.6g

Saturated Fat: 10.5g

Sodium: 745.8mg

Carbohydrates: 17g

Fiber: 5.1g

Sugar: 8g

Protein: 37.3g

Cholesterol: 168.9mg

## INGREDIENTS

*Meatballs*

1 pound lean ground chicken or turkey

1 cup shredded apple (about 1 large apple)

1 cup shredded sharp cheddar, divided

4 green onions, chopped

2 cloves garlic, minced

1 egg

Salt and pepper to season

*Salad*

3 slices thick cut bacon

1 large head broccoli, cut into small florets (about 5 cups of florets)

¼ cup light mayonnaise

¼ cup nonfat or low-fat plain Greek yogurt

1 tablespoon apple cider vinegar

1 teaspoon sugar

¼ teaspoon paprika

**APPLE CHEDDAR CHICKEN MEATBALLS:** Preheat oven to 375°F. Line a large rimmed baking sheet with foil for easy clean up and coat it with cooking spray. In a medium mixing bowl, combine the ground chicken, shredded apple, ½ cup shredded sharp cheddar, green onions, garlic, egg, and season with salt and pepper. Mix with your hands until the mixture is consistent. Form the meatball mix into 16 even-sized meatballs, each about the size of a golf ball. Bake for 20–25 minutes or until the meatballs are light brown throughout.

**BROCCOLI BACON SALAD:** In a medium skillet on medium heat, fry bacon until crisp. Drain on a paper towel to eliminate excess grease, and chop into fine pieces. Place broccoli florets in a medium serving bowl. In a small mixing bowl, combine the light mayonnaise, Greek yogurt, apple cider vinegar, sugar, and paprika. Whisk until a thick dressing forms. Pour over the broccoli and fold with a spoon to coat. Add the bacon and remaining ½ cup of shredded cheddar and toss again. Serve alongside the meatballs.

## CHANGE IT UP!
### Make a few changes to this recipe for two brand-new meals:

**CALIFORNIA MEATBALLS WITH SWEET BROCCOLI SALAD:**
Substitute blue cheese crumbles for the cheddar cheese and replace the bacon with ½ cup chopped sweetened dried cranberries.

**APPLE SWISS MEATBALLS WITH PEA SALAD:**
Substitute grated Swiss cheese for the cheddar cheese and replace the broccoli with one 16-ounce bag of frozen peas, thawed.

# OVEN-BAKED CHICKEN WINGS

Wings and pizza rank among my all-time favorite game-day or casual date night food. My husband would take a night out for wings and cold drafts over any fancy dinner. Since Bryan and I both love wings so much, I was determined to make a healthy recipe for those crispy, tasty bites of goodness. After many unsuccessful trials (my husband is a serious wing critic), Bryan approved! These wings are fantastic!

## NO MATTER WHICH OF MY YUMMY FLAVORS YOU CHOOSE, THESE THREE STEPS ARE ESSENTIAL FOR PERFECT OVEN WINGS:

1. Completely thaw your wings and dry them off *individually* with a paper towel. They must be completely dry.

2. Use a greased cooling rack over a rimmed, greased baking sheet to allow each wing to crisp up and bake completely. If you lay the wings directly on a baking sheet, they will be soggy.

3. Get out that baking powder and put it to use! Check out the recipes on the next 2 pages for more detailed directions.

# BUFFALO HOT WINGS

**PREP TIME:** 20 minutes    **BAKE TIME:** 30–35 minutes
**SERVINGS:** 6, 5 wings each
**TOTAL COST:** $11.34

## NUTRITIONAL INFORMATION

Calories: 355                Sodium: 2,476mg              Sugar: 0g
Total Fat: 25.4g             Carbohydrates: 2.6g          Protein: 24.4g
Saturated Fat: 7.9g          Fiber: 0.1g                  Cholesterol: 110.mg

## INGREDIENTS

*Wings*

4 pounds chicken wings (about 30 wings)
Salt and pepper to season
1 tablespoon baking powder, divided

*Sauce*

2 tablespoons butter
2 tablespoons flour
½ cup 99% fat free chicken broth
½ cup hot sauce (Red Hot is the best!)

## DIRECTIONS

**WINGS:** Preheat oven to 400°F. Spray 2 large rimmed baking sheets with cooking spray. Place 2 cooling racks that are just smaller than the baking sheets inside the baking sheets. Spray the cooling racks with cooking spray. Set aside.

Drain chicken wings in a strainer. Using dry paper towels, pat the wings dry, one at a time, and place in a separate container. Use a paring knife to trim any pieces of fat that are hanging off. Make sure the wings are thoroughly dried before continuing. Sprinkle 1 teaspoon baking powder all over the wings. Season with salt and pepper (about ¼ teaspoon of each). Toss the wings to coat using tongs. Repeat this process 2 times. Lay the wings out onto the cooling racks with at least ½ inch between each wing, about 15 wings per rack. Bake for 30–35 minutes or until the wings are crispy and completely cooked.

**WING SAUCE:** When 10 minutes remain on your timer, make the sauce. Melt 2 tablespoons of butter in a small saucepan over low heat. Whisk in 2 tablespoons of flour and cook for about 30 seconds, whisking constantly. Whisk in the hot sauce and chicken broth and bring to a simmer. Let the mixture cook and thicken for about 3–5 minutes, whisking frequently, until sauce thickens. When the wings are finished cooking, place them in a large bowl, pour the buffalo hot sauce over the wings, and toss with tongs to coat. Serve hot with celery and carrots.

# OLD BAY WINGS

While my husband's favorite wings are the Buffalo-style wings, Old Bay flavored wings rank as my favorite. Imagine a fried chicken wing married to a steamed Maryland blue crab. These wings are just superb.

**SERVINGS:** 6, 5 wings each
**TOTAL COST:** $10.38

## NUTRITIONAL INFORMATION

Calories: 354
Total Fat: 25g
Saturated Fat: 7.8g

Sodium: 571.1mg
Carbohydrates: 1.3g
Fiber: 0.1g

Sugar: 0.1g
Protein: 29.4g
Cholesterol: 116.8mg

Follow the wing recipe on the left (without the sauce), except add about 1 tablespoon Old Bay Seasoning. When you sprinkle the 1 teaspoon baking powder, also sprinkle 1 teaspoon Old Bay Seasoning. Toss to coat, and repeat 2 times.

---

# GARLIC PARMESAN WINGS

My dad and brother Ian prefer wings that match their Italian heritage. Garlic, salty parmesan cheese, and Italian seasonings are flavors that blend well and stick to the wings nicely.

**SERVINGS:** 6, 5 wings each
**TOTAL COST:** $10.82

## NUTRITIONAL INFORMATION

Calories: 321
Total Fat: 23g
Saturated Fat: 6.5g

Sodium: 906.7mg
Carbohydrates: 0.6g
Fiber: 0g

Sugar: 0g
Protein: 26.5g
Cholesterol: 111.5mg

Follow the wing recipe on the left (without the sauce), except add 1 ½ teaspoons dried Italian seasoning, ¾ teaspoon garlic powder, and ½ cup finely grated parmesan cheese (the "shaky" cheese in the canister works the best for this). When you sprinkle the 1 teaspoon baking powder, also sprinkle ½ teaspoon Italian seasoning and ¼ teaspoon garlic powder. Repeat 2 times. After the wings have baked, toss with parmesan.

# ITALIAN CHICKEN CUTLETS

Resist the temptation to buy chicken nuggets—are those fast food pieces of chicken even *real*? Wonder no more and spend your time making my aunt Gwen Berardinelli's amazing handheld chicken cutlets for dinner tonight. Kid and husband approved!

**PREP TIME:** 15 minutes     **BAKE TIME:** 15 minutes
**SERVINGS:** 6, about 2–3 filets each
***TOTAL COST:*** $8.98

## NUTRITIONAL INFORMATION

Calories: 225
Total Fat: 6.6g
Saturated Fat: 2.4g

Sodium: 446.2mg
Carbohydrates: 10.7g
Fiber: 0.8g

Sugar: 1g
Protein: 29.6g
Cholesterol: 98.6mg

## INGREDIENTS

¾ cup Italian seasoned breadcrumbs
¼ cup parmesan cheese
½ teaspoon dried parsley
½ teaspoon dried basil

Salt and pepper to season
1 egg, beaten
1 ½ pounds chicken breast tenderloins or
    chicken breast cut into thin filets

## DIRECTIONS

Preheat oven to 350°F. Place a cooling rack on top of a large rimmed baking sheet and spray with cooking spray. Take 2 shallow bowls and place them side by side next to the cooling rack-lined baking sheet. In one bowl, combine the breadcrumbs, parmesan cheese, parsley, and basil. Season the mix with salt and pepper and toss with your fingers to combine. In the next bowl, beat the egg very well. Season all of your chicken breast tenderloins or filets with salt and pepper. Dip each chicken piece completely in the egg then coat completely with the breadcrumb mixture. Lay the pieces out in an even layer on the cooling rack. Once all of the pieces are coated, bake for 15 minutes. Remove from the oven and serve with fresh tomatoes.

> The key to crispy cutlets is to create a "baking rack" so that the cutlets cook evenly and the breading doesn't get soggy.!

# BUFFALO GARLIC CROCK-POT CHICKEN

Wish you could have hot wings and pulled pork at the same time? This dish fits the bill. This Crock-Pot chicken recipe is not only great on a sandwich, but you can make a bulk amount of the recipe and use the leftovers in other dishes! It takes only about 10 minutes to assemble, and it's done by the time you're home from work.

**PREP TIME:** 10 minutes    **COOK TIME:** 8 hours on LOW
**SERVINGS:** 12, 4 ounces each
**TOTAL COST:** $12.57

## NUTRITIONAL INFORMATION

Calories: 148

Sodium: 661.7mg

Sugar: 0g

Total Fat: 3.1g

Carbohydrates: 2.5g

Protein: 26.1g

Saturated Fat: 0.8g

Fiber: 0.4g

Cholesterol: 70.2mg

## INGREDIENTS

1 large onion, sliced
1 head garlic cloves, peeled (about 7–8 cloves)
⅔ cup water
½ cup hot sauce, like Red Hot
3 pounds boneless skinless chicken breast (about 6 large breasts)
Salt and pepper to season

### Use This Recipe to Make:

Red Hot and Blue Sandwiches with Caramelized Onions, p. 124
Cheddar Chicken Tacos, p. 125
Buffalo Chicken Dip, p. 24
Buffalo Chicken Stromboli, p. 143

## DIRECTIONS

Combine sliced onions, whole cloves of garlic, water, and hot sauce in a large Crock-Pot. Season chicken breasts with salt and pepper and nestle them down into the sauce in the Crock-Pot. Cook on LOW for 8 hours. Remove the chicken to a big bowl for easy shredding. After shredding, add some of the pot juices to moisten if needed. Serve with a whole wheat pita half or sandwich bun.

# RED HOT AND BLUE SANDWICHES
## WITH CARAMELIZED ONIONS

**TOTAL TIME:** 35 minutes

**SERVINGS:** 6 sandwiches

**TOTAL COST:** $13.58

### NUTRITIONAL INFORMATION

Calories: 360

Total Fat: 11.3g

Saturated Fat: 4.3g

Sodium: 870mg

Carbohydrates: 31.1g

Fiber: 6.7g

Sugar: 3.1g

Protein: 35.5g

Cholesterol: 82.9mg

### INGREDIENTS

3 cups Buffalo Garlic Crock-Pot
    Chicken (p. 123)

2 medium onions, sliced (about 3 cups)

1 tablespoon olive oil

1 tablespoon balsamic vinegar

1 teaspoon sugar

6 whole wheat sandwich thins or burger buns

¾ cup blue cheese or gorgonzola, crumbled

### DIRECTIONS

Use the Buffalo Garlic Crock-Pot Chicken recipe on page 123 to make the chicken for this dish. It will take 8 hours in the Crock-Pot, so plan ahead! During the last 30 minutes of cook time for the chicken, make the caramelized onions. In a large skillet, combine sliced onions, 1 tablespoon olive oil, 1 tablespoon balsamic vinegar, and 1 teaspoon sugar. Cook over medium-low heat for about 30 minutes or until they are golden brown and caramelized, stirring occasionally. If you begin to see dark brown charring, turn down the heat. Remove from heat to cool.

Adjust the top oven rack to be 6 inches from the broiler. Preheat the broiler to HIGH. To build sandwiches, lay out the buns on a sturdy baking sheet. Pile ½ cup chicken onto the bottom bun. On top of the chicken, distribute the caramelized onions evenly among the 6 sandwiches. Sprinkle 2 tablespoons of blue cheese on the top of the onions. Broil 30 seconds to melt the cheese and remove from the oven. Top with the top bun and serve.

# CHEDDAR CHICKEN TACOS

**TOTAL TIME:** 20 minutes
**SERVINGS:** 6, 2 tacos each
**TOTAL COST:** $13.12

## NUTRITIONAL INFORMATION

Calories: 379

Total Fat: 16.8g

Saturated Fat: 7.8g

Sodium: 1,234.1mg

Carbohydrates: 19.3g

Fiber: 1.3g

Sugar: 4.5g

Protein: 34.6g

Cholesterol: 100.2mg

## INGREDIENTS

12 hard corn taco shells

3 cups Buffalo Garlic Crock-Pot Chicken (p. 123), or your choice of precooked chicken

1 ½ cups sharp cheddar cheese

3 cups lettuce, shredded

1 ½ cups salsa

## DIRECTIONS

If using Buffalo Garlic Crock-Pot Chicken, shred the chicken, measure out 3 cups for this recipe and refrigerate the remainder for another dish. If using chilled, precooked chicken, reheat in the microwave or a skillet until hot. Line up the taco shells and fill each with ¼ cup chicken, 2 tablespoons cheddar cheese, ¼ cup lettuce, and 2 tablespoons salsa. Serve immediately.

## NOT A FAN OF BUFFALO CHICKEN?

Turn to p. 128 and make Crock-Pot Pulled Pork to stuff these tacos instead!

# ITALIAN CHICKEN ROLL-UPS
## WITH CHRISTMAS PASTA

The holiday season is my favorite time to have a few friends over for some festive food and cheer. This meal takes less than an hour from start to finish, costs under $20 for 6 people, *and* it's only 510 calories per serving! Get ready to bring Christmas to your table with this budget- and waistline-friendly feast.

**TOTAL TIME:** 45 minutes
**SERVINGS:** 6, 2 chicken roll-ups and 1 cup of pasta each
*TOTAL COST:* $19.59

### NUTRITIONAL INFORMATION

Calories: 510
Total Fat: 17.8g
Saturated Fat: 5.7g

Sodium: 398.1mg
Carbohydrates: 38.2g
Fiber: 7.4g

Sugar: 2.3g
Protein: 49g
Cholesterol: 113.9mg

### INGREDIENTS

**Chicken Roll-Ups**

2 pounds thin-sliced chicken breast, 12 pieces in total
Salt and pepper to season
5 tablespoons basil pesto, divided
¾ cup ricotta or small curd cottage cheese
12 toothpicks
2 tablespoons olive oil

**Pasta**

8 ounces whole wheat short cut pasta, such as orecchiette or penne
1 pound green beans, trimmed and cut into 2 inch pieces
1 ½ cups cherry or grape tomatoes, halved
½ cup freshly grated parmesan cheese, plus more for serving if desired

## DIRECTIONS

### CHICKEN ROLL-UPS:

Preheat oven to 375°F. Lay out the chicken breasts in an even layer on a cookie sheet or plastic wrap. If you are using 4 regular chicken breasts, carefully cut each into 3 thin breasts to get 12 total. Season chicken with salt and pepper. Spoon 1 teaspoon of pesto onto each piece of chicken and spread evenly. Top pesto with 1 tablespoon ricotta cheese and spread evenly. Roll up the chicken breast and secure with a toothpick. Heat a large oven-proof

skillet over medium heat and add 2 tablespoons of olive oil. Season the chicken breast roll ups with salt and pepper and lay in the hot pan. Sear each of the 3 sides for 2 minutes until golden brown (6 minutes total). Place the pan in the hot oven and bake for 20 minutes.

**PASTA:** While your chicken bakes, prepare your pasta. Bring a pot of water to a boil. Add the pasta and season with salt. Set timer for amount of time recommended on package. When the pasta has 2 minutes of cook time remaining, add the trimmed green beans. Drain and place the pasta and green beans in a serving bowl. Add cherry tomato halves, remaining tablespoon of pesto, and ½ cup parmesan cheese, and toss to coat the pasta and vegetables completely. Season with salt and pepper.

Remove the cooked chicken roll-ups to a serving platter and pour any remaining liquid from the pan over the chicken. Serve the chicken roll-ups alongside the pasta.

# CROCK-POT PULLED PORK BBQ SANDWICHES

The Crock-Pot is a great tool to cut down on prep time and have a meal waiting for you when you arrive home on a busy day. This meal yields a lot of pork, making it a perfect choice for serving to large crowds when you are short on time.

**PREP TIME:** 7 minutes before cooking, plus 5 minutes before serving

**COOK TIME:** 8 hours on LOW

**SERVINGS:** 12 sandwiches, each with 4 ounces pulled pork

*TOTAL COST:* $15.50

## NUTRITIONAL INFORMATION

Calories: 390

Total Fat: 10.6g

Saturated Fat: 2.5g

Sodium: 707.2mg

Carbohydrates: 36.7g

Fiber: 5.5g

Sugar: 16.1g

Protein: 38.7g

Cholesterol: 90mg

## INGREDIENTS

1 tablespoon chili powder

1 tablespoon garlic powder

1 tablespoon cumin

1 tablespoon paprika

1 teaspoon salt

1 teaspoon freshly ground pepper

2 tablespoons brown sugar

3 pounds pork tenderloin, whole

1 cup chicken broth

1 cup BBQ sauce*

12 whole wheat sandwich thins or whole wheat burger buns

*Check out LBJ Barbeque Sauce (p. 236) or Sweet Garlic BBQ Sauce (p. 237) for a homemade sauce.*

## DIRECTIONS

Spray a 6–7-quart Crock-Pot with cooking spray. For the pork rub, combine the chili powder, garlic powder, cumin, paprika, salt, pepper, and brown sugar in a small bowl. Lay out the pork tenderloin on a large plastic cutting board and rub down completely with the chili rub. Place the seasoned pork into the Crock-Pot and pour in chicken broth around the outside edges of the pork.

Slow cook the pork on LOW for 7–8 hours. When finished, the liquid will be simmering and the pork should pull apart very easily with a fork. Remove the pork and place into a big bowl for easy shredding. After shredding, add some of the pot juices to moisten if needed.

Pour ¼ cup BBQ sauce over the shredded pork and stir to combine. Distribute pork evenly over the 12 burger buns and top with 1 more tablespoon of BBQ sauce on each sandwich.

## TIME AND MONEY-SAVING TIP:

This recipe makes 12 sandwiches, but I like to make 6 sandwiches with half of the pork and use the rest in my Pulled Pork Nachos recipe (p. 46) for second healthy meal!

## YUMMY VEGGIE PAIRINGS:

Twice-Baked Sweet Potatoes (p. 196), Crunchy Broccoli (p. 185), or Butternut Squash Fries (p. 186)

CROCK-POT PULLED
PORK BBQ SANDWICHES

# CROCK-POT PORK AND SAUERKRAUT

This is quite possibly the easiest dinner I have ever made! It takes 5 minutes to prepare in the morning and your Crock-Pot will do the cooking for you. With only 3 ingredients, you'll be hard-pressed to find a more simple and delicious dinner.

**PREP TIME:** 5 minutes    **COOK TIME:** 8 hours on LOW
**SERVINGS:** 8, 6 ounces of pork and ¾ cup sauerkraut each
*TOTAL COST:* $14.69

## NUTRITIONAL INFORMATION

Calories: 384

Sodium: 887.7mg

Sugar: 9g

Total Fat: 14.2g

Carbohydrates: 12.1g

Protein: 51.1g

Saturated Fat: 3.6g

Fiber: 3g

Cholesterol: 134.4mg

## INGREDIENTS

2 27-ounce cans sauerkraut
3 packed tablespoons brown sugar, divided
¼ teaspoon black pepper
3 pounds pork tenderloin, whole

## DIRECTIONS

Spray a large Crock-Pot with cooking spray to prevent sticking. Place the all of the contents of 1 can of sauerkraut in the bottom of your Crock-Pot. Sprinkle with 1 tablespoon brown sugar. Lay the pork tenderloin on top of the sauerkraut. Sprinkle black pepper and 1 tablespoon of brown sugar on top of the pork. Spread the remaining can of sauerkraut on top of the pork and sprinkle with the remaining 1 tablespoon of brown sugar. Place the lid on your Crock-Pot and cook on LOW for 8 hours.

# APPLE CIDER PORK CHOPS
## WITH APPLES AND ONIONS

Warm cider, apples, and sautéed onions are the best friends of pork chops. This recipe is perfect for fall when the weather starts to get chilly and apples are in season. I prefer boneless pork chops, but bone-in would substitute well.

**ACTIVE TIME:** 40 minutes    **MARINADE TIME:** 1 hour
**SERVINGS:** 6, 1 pork chop and ¾ cup of sautéed apples and onions each
*TOTAL COST:* $13.82

### NUTRITIONAL INFORMATION

Calories: 360
Total Fat: 12.5g
Saturated Fat: 5g

Sodium: 259mg
Carbohydrates: 28.5g
Fiber: 4.2g

Sugar: 19.4g
Protein: 32.3g
Cholesterol: 95mg

### INGREDIENTS

1 cup apple cider
2 tablespoons Dijon mustard
1 tablespoon fresh sage, chopped
1 tablespoon fresh thyme, chopped
3 tablespoon olive oil, divided
6 boneless pork chops, about 1 ½ pounds total
Salt and pepper to season

1 tablespoon butter
1 tablespoon flour
⅓ cup chicken broth
2 medium onions, sliced
6 medium apples, such as Golden Delicious, peeled, cored, and sliced ⅓-inch thick

## DIRECTIONS

In a large plastic bag, combine the apple cider, Dijon mustard, fresh sage, fresh thyme, and 1 tablespoon olive oil. Seal and shake to mix the marinade. Lay the pork chops out on a plate and season with salt and pepper on both sides. Use tongs to place the chops into the plastic bag. Let the meat marinade for 1 hour in the refrigerator.

In a large skillet, heat 1 tablespoon of olive oil over medium heat. Use the tongs to take the pork chops out of the bag and lay the chops in an even layer in the sauté pan. Do not discard the marinade. Sear the meat on each side for 2 minutes and then remove from the pan onto a clean plate. Melt 1 tablespoon of butter in the skillet and then whisk in the flour to create a roux. Let cook for about 30 seconds. Pour the reserved marinade into the skillet and whisk. Add the chicken broth and continue to whisk until slightly thickened. Remove ¼ cup of this sauce and reserve for the apples and onions. Add the pork chops back into the pan and reduce heat to medium-low. Simmer chops for 7–8 minutes. Flip them over to coat with sauce every few minutes.

While your pork cooks, prepare your apples and onions. In a separate large skillet, heat the remaining tablespoon of olive oil over medium heat. Cook sliced onions for 4–5 minutes or until they begin to soften. Add in the apples and season with salt and pepper. Cook the apples and onions for about 3 minutes. Fold in the ¼ cup of reserved pan sauce. Cook until the apples are tender to your liking, about 1–2 minutes longer or until your pork is finished cooking. Serve pork chops with the apples and onions. Spoon the remaining pan sauce over your meal if desired. Enjoy!

## PERFECT PAIRING!

Serve your meal with a salad of romaine lettuce, cubed apples, sweetened dried cranberries, and balsamic vinaigrette.

# PESTO PROSCIUTTO PIZZA

On a college visit to Rome, I was near St. Peter's Basilica when I had a slice of pizza with fresh pesto and prosciutto; it was the best pizza I'd ever tasted. I had to recreate that heavenly slice of Roman cuisine.

**PREP TIME:** 10 minutes    **BAKE TIME:** 20 minutes
**SERVINGS:** 6, 2 pieces each
*TOTAL COST:* $9.27

### NUTRITIONAL INFORMATION

Calories: 378

Total Fat: 20.6g

Saturated Fat: 6.3g

Sodium: 1,004mg

Carbohydrates: 32.9g

Fiber: 5.4g

Sugar: 2.6g

Protein: 17.3g

Cholesterol: 33.3mg

### INGREDIENTS

1 pound store-bought whole wheat pizza dough (or see p. 84 to make your own)
½ cup prepared pesto (or see p. 234 to make your own)
1 cup mozzarella or Italian blend cheese, grated
½ cup Pecorino Romano cheese
4 ounces prosciutto, chopped or pulled into small pieces

### DIRECTIONS

Preheat oven to 400°F. Spray a large rimmed baking sheet, about 15x10 inches, with cooking spray. Roll out the pizza dough to fit the size of the baking sheet. Spread the pesto evenly over the dough. Sprinkle the cheeses evenly over the pesto, and top with prosciutto pieces. Bake for 20 minutes or until the crust is golden brown on the bottom. Cut into 12 pieces and serve with a side salad.

# GRILLED TURKEY KIELBASA
## WITH CHARRED BELL PEPPERS

I absolutely love biting into a piece of kielbasa right off the grill or roasted over a fire. Forget the bun and hand over the mustard, a fork, and a knife! The flavor of grilled bell peppers is the perfect accompaniment for kielbasa. If you don't have a grill or it's a little too cold outside, get out a grill pan! You can pick them up at your local kitchen store for about $30. But, if it's summer, fire up your grill to make this amazing meal.

**TOTAL TIME:** 20 minutes
**SERVINGS:** 6, 1 kielbasa and 8 pepper slices each
*TOTAL COST:* $9.79

### NUTRITIONAL INFORMATION

| | | |
|---|---|---|
| Calories: 231 | Sodium: 1,107mg | Sugar: 2.2g |
| Total Fat: 12.5g | Carbohydrates: 12g | Protein: 20.3g |
| Saturated Fat: 0.2g | Fiber: 3.4g | Cholesterol: 65mg |

### INGREDIENTS

3 bell peppers, each cut into 16 slices
2 teaspoons olive oil
⅛ teaspoon salt
⅛ teaspoon black pepper
2 13-ounce packages turkey kielbasa, cut into 3 pieces each
Mustard for serving, optional

### DIRECTIONS

Heat an outdoor grill or indoor grill pan over medium heat. Toss the pepper slices with olive oil, salt, and pepper. Once the grill is hot, lay kielbasa pieces on one side of the grill and the pepper slices on another side. Grill for 10–12 minutes, turning the peppers and kielbasa occasionally to cook evenly. Remove from the grill to place on a serving platter. Serve with mustard if desired.

# SPAGHETTI SQUASH CARBONARA

I fell in love with pasta carbonara on a college visit to Rome. It was velvety and flavorful, but also very heavy. I've lightened up this Italian favorite using spaghetti squash and half and half cream as my secret ingredients. The traditional flavors are still very prominent in this veggie-packed entrée, so you won't miss the heavy cream sauce and pasta. Top this delicious entrée with chicken or shrimp for added protein.

**TOTAL TIME:** 50–60 minutes
**SERVINGS:** 6, about 1 ⅓ cup each
*TOTAL COST:* $9.44

## NUTRITIONAL INFORMATION

| | | |
|---|---|---|
| Calories: 290 | Sodium: 384.4mg | Sugar: 7.8g |
| Total Fat: 17.4g | Carbohydrates: 20.6g | Protein: 13.9g |
| Saturated Fat: 8.1g | Fiber: 2.7g | Cholesterol: 125.9mg |

## INGREDIENTS

2 small or 1 large spaghetti squash, about 4 pounds total
2 tablespoons olive oil, divided
Salt and pepper
3 medium or 1 extra large sweet onion, sliced (about 2 cups)
1 teaspoon sugar
1 tablespoon balsamic vinegar

4 slices thick cut bacon
¼ cup flour
1 cup half and half
1 cup low-fat milk
3 eggs
½ cup parmesan cheese, grated
¼ cup fresh parsley, finely chopped

## DIRECTIONS

Preheat oven to 400°F. Line a rimmed baking sheet with foil and spray with cooking spray. To prepare the spaghetti squash for baking, cut it in half lengthwise. Scoop out all of the seeds and loose flesh inside. Drizzle 1 tablespoon olive oil over the cut side of the spaghetti squash halves and season with salt and pepper. Spread evenly with your finger. Roast cut side down for 45–55 minutes (time will depend on the size of your squash) or until you can squeeze the squash with your oven mitt and the strands of the squash come away from the skin easily when pulled with a fork. Let cool for 5 minutes and then use a fork to pull out strands of squash from the skin into a large serving bowl.

While the spaghetti squash roasts, heat 1 tablespoon of olive oil in a large skillet over medium-low heat. Add sliced onions, sugar, and balsamic vinegar. Stir to coat evenly and cook onions over low heat until golden brown and caramelized, about 30 minutes. Stir occasionally to prevent burning.

In a separate pan, fry bacon slices over medium heat until crispy. Crumble the bacon and set aside. Reserve 2 tablespoons of the bacon grease in the pan to build the sauce. If you use a leaner bacon, you may not get 2 full tablespoons of bacon grease; add olive oil to reach 2 full tablespoons if needed. Turn heat down to medium-low. Sprinkle the flour over the bacon drippings and whisk together to form a roux. Cook for about 1 minute and then slowly drizzle the milk and half and half into the pan, whisking constantly. Bring the mixture to steaming, but not boiling. Whisk the eggs in a separate bowl and then whisk about ⅓ cup of the hot milk mixture into the eggs to temper them. Add the egg mixture slowly to the pan sauce, whisking constantly. When the sauce thickens slightly, sprinkle in the parmesan cheese and continue to whisk until the cheese melts. Season with salt and pepper.

Pour the carbonara sauce over the strands of spaghetti squash in the serving bowl and top with caramelized onions and bacon crumbles. Gently stir the mixture to combine all of the flavors together. Garnish with chopped parsley, and serve hot.

# CURRY TURKEY STUFFED PEPPERS

My grandfather, Paul Bucci, kept one of the most organized and fruitful gardens I've ever seen. He always had a plethora of peppers that my mom would stuff with meat and rice. This is my own version of her stuffed peppers that take just one hour to hit the table.

**PREP TIME:** 35 minutes  **BAKE TIME:** 25 minutes
**SERVINGS:** 8 stuffed peppers
*TOTAL COST:* $13.58

## NUTRITIONAL INFORMATION

Calories: 246          Sodium: 590.1mg          Sugar: 0.7g
Total Fat: 12g          Carbohydrates: 17.5g          Protein: 18.4g
Saturated Fat: 4.3g          Fiber: 2g          Cholesterol: 52.4mg

## INGREDIENTS

1 cup water
1 teaspoon curry powder
¼ teaspoon salt
1 cup instant brown rice, dry
1 tablespoon olive oil
1 medium onion, chopped
3 cloves garlic, minced
½ pound lean ground turkey
½ pound turkey sausage

Salt and pepper to season
1 cup corn
1 medium tomato, chopped
¼ cup fresh parsley, chopped
1 cup mozzarella or Italian cheese, shredded and divided
½ cup parmesan cheese, shredded or grated
4 large bell peppers, any color

## SIMPLIFY:

Use 1 pound of either lean ground turkey or turkey sausage rather than ½ pound of each.

## DIRECTIONS

Bring 1 cup of water, 1 teaspoon of curry powder, and ¼ teaspoon of salt to a simmer in a small saucepan. Add the brown rice. Follow the package directions on the rice. Usually you simmer with a lid on for 5 minutes and then remove from heat and let the pan sit for 5 additional minutes. Don't take off the lid!

Preheat oven to 400°F. In a large sauté skillet, heat 1 tablespoon olive oil over medium heat. Add onions and garlic and sauté until soft, about 3–4 minutes, stirring occasionally. Add the ground turkey and turkey sausage. Season with salt and pepper and stir to combine, breaking up the chunks of turkey and sausage. Cook until the turkey is fully browned. Add in the corn, tomato, parsley, and cooked rice mixture. Stir to combine. Remove from heat and stir in ½ cup mozzarella or Italian cheese and ½ cup parmesan cheese and season with salt and pepper (about ¼ teaspoon each). Let cool while you clean your peppers.

**Bell peppers are packed with beta-carotene, Vitamin C, and potassium!**

Coat a 13x9 baking dish with cooking spray. Cut each pepper in half lengthwise. Discard the seeds, stem, and additional white ribbing inside the pepper. Lay the peppers inside the baking dish, cut side up. Fill each pepper half with the turkey-rice mixture until you have used all of the filling. Use your fingers to gently press the mixture down into the pepper if necessary. Top the peppers with the remaining ½ cup of mozzarella or Italian cheese. Bake for about 25 minutes or until the peppers are soft and the cheese is melted.

# LIGHTENED-UP LASAGNA

Lasagna is the perfect make-ahead dinner for a crowd. My best friend, Erin, taught me how to make lasagna in college, and it lasted us all week! Since then, I've added a few of my own healthy and time-saving twists to the recipe to make it my own delicious dinner for a dozen. No need to boil the oven-ready noodles or make a time-consuming sauce.

**PREP TIME:** 30 minutes    **BAKE TIME:** 45 minutes
**SERVINGS:** 12 pieces of lasagna
**TOTAL COST:** $13.03

## NUTRITIONAL INFORMATION

Calories: 285

Total Fat: 11.5g

Saturated Fat: 5.1g

Sodium: 680.7mg

Carbohydrates: 23.7g

Fiber: 2g

Sugar: 6g

Protein: 23.8g

Cholesterol: 50.2mg

## INGREDIENTS

1 tablespoon olive oil

1 medium onion, chopped

3 garlic cloves, minced

1 pound lean ground turkey

Salt and pepper to season

23.5-ounce jar of light spaghetti sauce, such as Prego Light Smart

8-ounce can of tomato sauce with Italian herbs

16 ounces part-skim ricotta cheese

2 cups low-fat, small curd cottage cheese

½ cup parmesan cheese

1 teaspoon dried basil

1 teaspoon dried parsley

1 teaspoon dried oregano

12 oven-ready lasagna noodles, uncooked

1 cup part-skim mozzarella cheese, shredded

## DIRECTIONS

In a large skillet, sauté olive oil, onions, and garlic over medium heat until onions are translucent, about 4 minutes. Add ground turkey and season with salt and pepper. Sauté until browned. Add in the spaghetti sauce and tomato sauce and bring to a simmer for about 5 minutes.

In a separate medium bowl, combine the ricotta cheese, cottage cheese, parmesan cheese, basil, parsley and oregano. Stir to combine and season with salt and pepper to taste.

Preheat oven to 375°F. In a greased 13x9 baking dish, ladle a few spoonfuls of the meat sauce and spread evenly over the bottom of the pan. Lay 4 noodles on top of the sauce, breaking off the ends if needed, to make the noodles fit evenly in 1 layer. Spread ⅓ of the cheese mixture over the dry noodles. Scoop ⅓ of the remaining sauce mixture on top of the cheese. Repeat these noodle-cheese-sauce layers 2 more times until all of the noodles, cheese, and sauce are used. Your top layer should be sauce. Sprinkle the top layer evenly with mozzarella cheese.

Cover with foil and bake for 30 minutes at 375°F. Uncover and bake an additional 15 minutes. The lasagna is done when a knife can cut through the layers easily. Let stand for 5 minutes before serving. Serve with my Easy Cheesy Garlic Bread (p. 82).

# LAUREN K'S SICILIAN STROMBOLI

Everyone I know *loves* my Stromboli recipe, including *The Rachael Ray Show*! I always use this recipe to show my students at Penn Cambria how to make healthy substitutions. Seeing that so many teenagers loved it, I decided to demonstrate it for my video application for The Rachael Ray Great American Cookbook Competition. It certainly caught their attention and has become a community and national favorite.

**PREP TIME:** 25 minutes    **BAKE TIME:** 20 minutes
**SERVINGS:** 6
**TOTAL COST:** $8.62

## NUTRITIONAL INFORMATION

Calories: 405                Sodium: 1,213mg             Sugar: 0.8g
Total Fat: 17.5g             Carbohydrates: 35g          Protein: 27.5g
Saturated Fat: 6.4g          Fiber: 5.8g                 Cholesterol: 65.3mg

## INGREDIENTS

1 tablespoon olive oil                    4 large slices deli ham
1 medium onion, chopped                   ½ cup parmesan cheese, grated
3 cloves garlic, minced                   ½ cup Italian cheese (mozzarella or Italian
8 ounces turkey sausage                       blend), grated
1 pound store-bought whole wheat pizza    30 slices turkey pepperoni
    dough (or see p. 84 to make your own)  1 egg, beaten
1 teaspoon dried parsley                  Tomato sauce for serving, optional
1 teaspoon dried basil

## DIRECTIONS

Preheat oven to 400°F. Spray a large rimmed baking sheet with cooking spray.

Preheat a large skillet to medium heat. Add 1 tablespoon of olive oil, onions, and garlic and sauté for 3–4 minutes, until onions are translucent. Add turkey sausage, breaking it up into bite-sized pieces, and sauté until browned. Remove from heat to cool.

On the large rimmed baking sheet, roll out the pizza dough to fit the length of the baking sheet. Sprinkle the surface of the dough with parsley and basil. Lay the ham down the middle of the dough. Sprinkle the parmesan cheese evenly over the ham. Next, layer on the turkey sausage mixture, Italian cheese, and turkey pepperoni. Once the fillings are added, take one long side of the dough and gently pull it over the filling. Repeat with the other side so that all of the filling is covered. It should look like a giant burrito. Fold up the ends of the dough and seal edges by pressing lightly. Cut 3 small vent holes in the top of the Stromboli to allow for steam to escape. Use a basting brush to brush the surface of the uncooked Stromboli with the beaten egg. Bake for 20 minutes until the top crust is golden brown. Let it rest for 5 minutes before serving. Slice with a large knife or pizza cutter and serve with warm tomato sauce on the side, if desired. A side salad of romaine, tomatoes, and cucumbers is a great pairing.

## CHANGE IT UP!

You can make all of the variations below with this recipe. All you need is a type of cheese and the pizza dough. Just make sure all of your ingredients are fully cooked before you bake the Stromboli.

**BUFFALO CHICKEN STROMBOLI:** Sautéed onions, garlic, and celery with cooked chicken, hot sauce, and blue cheese

**BREAKFAST STROMBOLI:** Scrambled eggs, cooked bacon, green onions, and cheddar cheese

**BBQ CHICKEN STROMBOLI:** Grilled chicken tossed in BBQ sauce, sautéed red onions, and cheddar cheese

**PHILLY STEAK AND CHEESE STROMBOLI:** Grilled steak, provolone cheese, sautéed green peppers, mushrooms, and onions

# MINI PEPPER PIZZAS

American families often seek out pizza for a quick weeknight dinner, but pizza delivery usually takes 45 minutes to arrive and costs about $20. These pepper "pizzas" add a yummy vegetable to your dinner for a meal that is under $10 for a family of 5. Pair with whole wheat garlic bread for a secretly healthy meal that everyone in your family will love to eat when it's finished in 30 minutes.

**TOTAL TIME:** 30 minutes
**SERVINGS:** 5, 7–8 pepper pizzas each
*TOTAL COST:* $9.34

## NUTRITIONAL INFORMATION

Calories: 170

Total Fat: 6.8g

Saturated Fat: 3.8g

Sodium: 756.4mg

Carbohydrates: 17g

Fiber: 3.6g

Sugar: 2.8g

Protein: 13.2g

Cholesterol: 32mg

## INGREDIENTS

1-pound bag of mini yellow, red, or orange bell peppers, about 18 mini peppers per bag, about 2–3 inches each

1 cup light spaghetti sauce, such as Prego Light Smart

1 cup Italian blend or mozzarella cheese, shredded

½ cup parmesan cheese, shredded

25 slices turkey pepperoni, chopped

Salt and pepper to season

## DIRECTIONS

Preheat oven to 400°F and coat a large rimmed baking sheet lightly with olive oil spray. Wash the peppers and cut each one in half lengthwise. Use your fingers to remove and discard the seeds and stems. Lay the peppers skin side down in an even layer on the baking sheet. Spoon the spaghetti sauce inside each pepper. Sprinkle the Italian and parmesan cheeses on top of the sauce. Top each with a pinch of chopped turkey pepperoni. Season the pizzas lightly with salt and pepper. Bake for about 12–13 minutes or until the cheese is fully melted and begins to brown and bubble. Serve immediately.

# ZUCCHINI PIZZAS

The first harvest in many Pennsylvania gardens yields an abundance of zucchini. Since I love both pizza and zucchini, I merged the two into a yummy quick and easy fork-and-knife pizza dinner! It's low in carbohydrates and sugar, but packed with fiber and calcium. The big zucchinis work best for this recipe. Feel free to add your own favorite pizza toppings, like mushrooms, onions, or peppers, for a fun twist.

**PREP TIME:** 20 minutes     **BAKE TIME:** 20–23 minutes
**SERVINGS:** 6
*TOTAL COST:* $7.02

## NUTRITIONAL INFORMATION

Calories: 185

Total Fat: 8.6g

Saturated Fat: 4g

Sodium: 793.9mg

Carbohydrates: 18.6g

Fiber: 4.5g

Sugar: 9.9g

Protein: 12.7g

Cholesterol: 33.3mg

## INGREDIENTS

1 extra large zucchini, 2 large, or 3 medium zucchini, unpeeled

14 ounces pizza or spaghetti sauce (about 1 ¾ cups)

1 ½ cups Italian blend cheese

34 slices turkey pepperoni

## DIRECTIONS

Preheat oven to 400°F. Cut the zucchini into ½-inch slices and lay out on a large rimmed baking sheet sprayed with cooking spray. Spread the pizza sauce evenly over all of the zucchini slices. Top with the Italian cheese and turkey pepperoni. Bake the pizzas for 20–23 minutes, or until the cheese is bubbly and beginning to brown. Serve hot.

**MAKE IT AN APPETIZER!**
Follow the directions for this recipe, but use 5 small-sized zucchinis, about 6–7 inches in length. Serve as bite-sized snacks to your guests.

# HARVEST STUFFED ACORN SQUASH

Acorn squash is one of my favorite vegetables. Its creamy texture and beautiful presentation will invite anyone into the world of healthy eating. The turkey sausage, fruit, and nut filling can be prepared as your acorn squash roasts in the oven so you can have an impressive dinner on the table with no stress!

**BAKE TIME:** 45 minutes    **ACTIVE TIME:** 25 minutes
**SERVINGS:** 6, 1 stuffed squash half each
*TOTAL COST:* $12.94

## NUTRITIONAL INFORMATION

Calories: 420

Sodium: 647.5mg

Sugar: 18.9g

Total Fat: 22.2g

Carbohydrates: 48.6g

Protein: 17.5g

Saturated Fat: 3.7g

Fiber: 6.5g

Cholesterol: 50.4mg

## INGREDIENTS

3 medium acorn squash, about 4 inches each
3 tablespoons olive oil, divided
Salt and pepper to season
1 medium onion, chopped
1 pound turkey sausage, casings removed
2 medium golden delicious apples, cut into ½-inch cubes
½ cup sweetened dried cranberries
½ cup 99% fat free chicken broth
½ cup walnuts or pecans, roughly chopped
2 tablespoons maple syrup
1 tablespoon balsamic vinegar

> In my family, we call this dish the "Witches' Cauldrons" because we usually make it as Halloween approaches.

## DIRECTIONS

Preheat oven to 400°F. Line a rimmed baking sheet with foil and spray with cooking spray to prevent sticking. Cut the acorn squash in half through the stem. Remove the seeds with a sturdy spoon. Drizzle 1 teaspoon of olive oil into each squash and season with salt and pepper. Spread the olive oil, salt, and pepper around the fleshy side of the squash with your fingers. Lay cut side down and roast for 40–45 minutes, or until the squash is soft when squeezed with an oven mitt. Remove from the oven and cool slightly.

When the squash has about 15 minutes remaining, heat 1 tablespoon of olive oil in a large skillet over medium heat. Add onions and sauté for about 3 minutes. Add the turkey sausage to the cooking onions, breaking up the chunks of sausage into small pieces. Cook until the sausage is browned and the onions are translucent, about 5 more minutes. Add the apples, cranberries, and chicken broth to the sausage and bring to a simmer for about 3 minutes, until the mixture begins to thicken. Add the nuts, maple syrup, and balsamic vinegar. Stir to combine and cook for about 1 minute longer. Season with salt and pepper.

When the squash is done baking, place the halves on a serving dish, cut side up. Spoon the sausage mixture into the squash halves. Serve warm.

# "SPAGHETTI" AND MEATBALLS

Spaghetti and meatballs rank among my husband's all-time favorite dinners. However, in an effort to lose a few pounds, he challenged me to make a low-carb version of his desired dinner staple. My friend Leslie had introduced me to spaghetti squash, and I knew I had to give it a try with this dish. This classic Italian pair will leave you full and satisfied. *Mangia!*

**TOTAL TIME:** 50 minutes
**SERVINGS:** 4 entrées, each with 4 meatballs, 1 ½ cups squash, and 1 tablespoon parmesan cheese
*TOTAL COST:* $13.26

## NUTRITIONAL INFORMATION

| | | |
|---|---|---|
| Calories: 443 | Sodium: 1,606mg | Sugar: 20.5g |
| Total Fat: 16.2g | Carbohydrates: 44.3g | Protein: 33.6g |
| Saturated Fat: 5.7g | Fiber: 9.8g | Cholesterol: 136.4mg |

## INGREDIENTS

1 large spaghetti squash, about 3 pounds
2 teaspoons olive oil
Salt and pepper to season
1 pound lean ground turkey
½ small onion, finely chopped
2–3 cloves garlic, minced
1 egg
¼ cup Italian breadcrumbs
1 tablespoon fresh chopped basil (or 1 teaspoon dried)
1 tablespoon fresh chopped parsley (or 1 teaspoon dried)
½ teaspoon garlic powder
4 cups of spaghetti sauce, such as Prego Light Smart
½ cup parmesan cheese, grated and divided

## DIRECTIONS

Preheat oven to 375°F. Line a rimmed baking sheet with foil and coat with cooking spray. To prepare the spaghetti squash for baking, cut it in half lengthwise. Scoop out all of the seeds and loose flesh inside using a sturdy spoon. Drizzle 1 teaspoon of olive oil over the flesh of each of the spaghetti squash halves, season with salt and pepper, and spread with your fingers to evenly coat the entire fleshy portion of the squash. Roast cut side down for 40–50 minutes or until you can squeeze the squash with an oven mitt and the strands of the squash come away from the skin easily when pulled with a fork. After the squash is cooked, let cool for 5 minutes. Using an oven mitt, hold the spaghetti squash half and use a fork to pull out strands of squash into a serving bowl. Repeat with the second squash half.

While the squash cooks, prepare the meatballs. Line a rimmed baking sheet with foil and coat with cooking spray. In a medium mixing bowl, combine ground turkey, onion, garlic, egg, breadcrumbs, basil, parsley, and garlic powder. Season the mixture with salt and pepper. Using your hand, combine all the ingredients together well. Form golf ball-sized meatballs (16 total) and lay on the prepared baking sheet with at least ½ inch of space between each meatball. Put these in the oven when there is 15 minutes remaining for the spaghetti squash. Cook for 20–25 minutes total, or until the meatballs are brown throughout.

After the squash and meatballs are in the oven, heat all 4 cups of spaghetti sauce in a medium saucepan over medium heat. Once the sauce is warm and the spaghetti squash is done and pulled into strands, mix about 2 cups of spaghetti sauce into the squash. Stir to coat the squash with sauce. Season with salt and pepper and stir in ¼ cup parmesan cheese. Reserve the remaining 2 cups of sauce in the pan for the meatballs.

**Pick organic or no-sugar-added tomato sauce to avoid harmful food additives, like high fructose corn syrup.**

When the meatballs are brown throughout, remove from the oven and add them to the remaining 2 cups of hot spaghetti sauce in the saucepan. Fold gently to coat them in sauce. Serve the spaghetti squash as the "spaghetti" and top with meatballs and 1 tablespoon of parmesan cheese per serving.

# BEEF "GYROS"
## WITH GREEK SALAD

Gyros definitely rank among my husband's favorite festival foods. With all of the Greek flavors, crunchy veggies, and delicious cucumber sauce wrapped in a soft pita, this handheld favorite is hard to beat. Lamb, however, can be quite pricey, so I came up with a beef version that is very simple and quick, but just as tasty. A Greek salad side dish not only completes the meal, but also uses some leftover gyro ingredients, thus saving you money, too!

**TOTAL TIME:** 30 minutes
**SERVINGS:** 5, each with 1 pita and 1 heaping cup of salad
**TOTAL COST:** $16.83

## NUTRITIONAL INFORMATION

Calories: 431
Total Fat: 21.1g
Saturated Fat: 6.2g

Sodium: 1,145mg
Carbohydrates: 22.3g
Fiber: 7.5g

Sugar: 5.2g
Protein: 42.4g
Cholesterol: 94mg

## INGREDIENTS

3 tablespoon olive oil, divided
1 medium onion, sliced
3 cloves garlic, minced
1 pound lean ground beef or thinly sliced lean steak, such as sirloin
3 teaspoons Greek seasoning, such as Cavender, divided
¾ cup plain Greek yogurt
¼ cup sour cream
Juice of ½ lemon
1 large cucumber, peeled, seeded, and divided
5 whole wheat pita halves or 5 thin pita breads, such as Joseph's
1 large head iceberg or romaine lettuce, chopped and divided
3 medium tomatoes, diced and divided
3 tablespoons red wine vinegar
½ cup feta cheese crumbles

## DIRECTIONS

**GYRO:** In a large skillet, heat 1 tablespoon of olive oil over medium heat. Add the onions and garlic and sauté for 4 minutes until soft. Add in ground beef or sliced steak and season with 1 teaspoon of Greek seasoning. Cook for about 4 minutes, stirring occasionally, until the beef is done to your liking (if using ground beef, cook until fully browned). Keep warm until ready to serve.

For the cucumber sauce, combine the plain Greek yogurt, sour cream, lemon juice, 1 teaspoon Greek seasoning, ⅛ teaspoon salt, and ⅛ teaspoon pepper in a small bowl. Cut the cucumber into thirds and set aside ⅓ of the cucumber for the salad. Finely chop the remaining ⅔ of the cucumber and stir into the yogurt sauce. Set aside until ready to serve.

To build the gyros, open each pita half and gently layer ⅕ of the cooked beef, ¼ cup lettuce, and 2 tablespoons tomatoes inside. Top with 3 tablespoons of cucumber sauce each. Serve with 1 heaping cup of Greek Salad per person.

**GREEK SALAD:** Roughly chop ¾ of the lettuce head and place in a large serving bowl. Add 2 diced tomatoes and remaining ⅓ cucumber, cut in half-moon shapes. In a small bowl, combine 2 tablespoons olive oil, 3 tablespoons red wine vinegar, and the remaining 1 teaspoon of Greek seasoning. Pour over the salad and toss to coat. Top with feta cheese crumbles.

# ITALIAN PAISAN BURGERS

I always remember hearing my dad call his Italian buddies *paisan*, which means "friend" in Italian. These burgers were inspired by my Italian heritage and the fun times my family has shared surrounded by pesto, tomatoes, and melted cheese. These burgers will not only bring your "friends" back for seconds at your next gathering, but they are budget and waistline "friendly" as well! Serve with grilled asparagus or green beans for a complete meal.

**TOTAL TIME:** 30 minutes
**SERVINGS:** 8 burgers
*TOTAL COST:* $12.66

## NUTRITIONAL INFORMATION

| | | |
|---|---|---|
| Calories: 416 | Sodium: 640.1mg | Sugar: 3.3g |
| Total Fat: 21.1g | Carbohydrates: 24.7g | Protein: 30g |
| Saturated Fat: 6.1g | Fiber: 2.7g | Cholesterol: 93.3mg |

## INGREDIENTS

*Burger Patties*
1 pound lean ground beef (93/7 ratio of lean meat to fat)
½ pound turkey sausage, removed from casings
¼ cup onion, finely chopped
2 cloves garlic, minced
¼ teaspoon dried oregano
¼ teaspoon dried basil
¼ teaspoon garlic powder
¼ teaspoon salt
¼ teaspoon pepper
1 egg

*Toppings and Buns*
½ cup prepared pesto
8 ounces fresh mozzarella, sliced into 8 slices (sliced mozzarella from your deli works great too)
2 tomatoes, sliced into 4 slices each
8 whole wheat burger buns

## DIRECTIONS

Heat an outdoor grill to medium or indoor grill pan to medium heat over a stove range. If grilling the burgers on a grill pan, you may need to work in 2 batches.

To make the burger patties, combine the ground beef, turkey sausage, onion, garlic, oregano, basil, garlic powder, salt, pepper, and egg. Mix thoroughly with your hands until all ingredients are thoroughly combined and the mixture looks uniform throughout. Form into 8 thin patties.

Grill patties for 4 minutes on the first side, flip, and grill for 3 minutes on the second side. Spoon 1 tablespoon of pesto on each patty and top with 1 slice of mozzarella cheese. Grill for an additional 1–2 minutes or until the cheese is melted and the burgers are cooked through. Remove from the grill and let rest for 2 minutes. Lay burgers on buns and top with a slice of tomato.

> ## TIP:
> Make the patties thinner in the middle before cooking because they will expand in the center as they cook on the grill.

## TRY A NEW BURGER!

**BUFFALO TURKEY BURGER:** Replace the beef and turkey sausage with ground turkey and omit the oregano and basil. Top with 8 ounces of blue cheese mixed with ¼ cup hot sauce.

**PHILLY STEAK AND CHEESE BURGER:** Replace the pesto, mozzarella, and tomatoes with sautéed onions and bell peppers. Top with sliced provolone cheese.

# MOM AND DAD'S LONDON BROIL
## WITH ROASTED GARLIC GREEN BEANS

My mom is the master cook at home, but sometimes my parents put their heads and hands together to feed large crowds. For this recipe, my mom always makes the marinade and the sides and my dad cooks and slices the meat. No matter how many times I try to replicate it, I just can't make it *quite* as good as they can. Maybe it takes the love of two people to make this dish just right. Grab your significant other or a friend to make and eat this meaty main dish together!

**MARINADE TIME:** 24–48 hours    **COOK TIME:** 20 minutes
**SERVINGS:** 6, each with 5 ounces of beef and 1 cup of green beans
**TOTAL COST:** $19.85

## NUTRITIONAL INFORMATION

Calories: 395

Total Fat: 6.5g

Saturated Fat: 0.5g

Sodium: 653.4mg

Carbohydrates: 17.1g

Fiber: 2.9g

Sugar: 9g

Protein: 55.7g

Cholesterol: 135mg

## INGREDIENTS

*London Broil*
¼ cup maple syrup
¼ cup low-sodium soy sauce
½ cup red wine
3 cloves of garlic, minced
1 teaspoon cinnamon
½ teaspoon freshly cracked black pepper
Salt and pepper to season
2 pound London broil or flank steak

*Roasted Garlic Green Beans*
2 pounds of green beans, ends trimmed
1 teaspoon butter
Salt and pepper to season
1 tablespoon Roasted Garlic (see p. 238)

---

## DIRECTIONS

**LONDON BROIL:** In a large sealable plastic bag, combine the maple syrup, soy sauce, red wine, garlic, cinnamon, and cracked black pepper for the marinade. Generously season the London broil on both sides with salt and pepper. Place the seasoned meat into the marinade bag and toss a few times to coat. Refrigerate for 24–48 hours, flipping the meat over every 12 hours if possible, to allow the marinade to infuse flavor to all sides. Bring to room temperature before cooking.

Preheat broiler to HIGH. Line a thick rimmed baking sheet with foil and spray with cooking spray. Take the meat out of the bag. Do not discard the marinade! Broil the meat on each side for about 8 minutes per side for medium doneness—more or less depending on how you like your steak cooked. Remove from the broiler and let rest for 10 minutes. Slice against the grain of the meat for a tender bite.

While the steak cooks, heat the marinade in a small saucepan. Simmer 5 minutes and use as a sauce for the steak.

**GARLIC GREEN BEANS:** While the steak rests, place the green beans and ¼ cup of water in a large microwave-safe bowl. Cover with a lid or tightly with plastic wrap. Microwave on high for 4 minutes. Carefully remove the lid or plastic wrap and drain the excess water. Place in a large serving bowl and toss with 1 teaspoon butter, salt, pepper, and 1 tablespoon of Roasted Garlic. Serve hot.

# REUBEN POCKETS
## *WITH HOMEMADE THOUSAND ISLAND DRESSING*

A Reuben sandwich is my favorite bistro classic. Deli pastrami, sliced Swiss cheese, and store-bought pizza dough make this a quick and easy meal to put together. The homemade Thousand Island dressing will put a gourmet twist on these pockets with some pantry and refrigerator staples.

**TOTAL TIME:** 35 minutes
**SERVINGS:** 6, 1 pocket with 2 tablespoons dressing
***TOTAL COST:*** $10.24

### NUTRITIONAL INFORMATION

Calories: 367

Total Fat: 14.1g

Saturated Fat: 5.8g

Sodium: 1,344mg

Carbohydrates: 37.1g

Fiber: 5.6g

Sugar: 4.7g

Protein: 20.7g

Cholesterol: 48.7mg

### INGREDIENTS

*Reuben Pockets*

1 pound whole wheat pizza dough (see p. 84 for a homemade recipe)

Flour for dusting

½ pound deli pastrami

⅓ pound sliced Swiss cheese (about 6 slices)

1 cup sauerkraut, drained and squeezed of excess liquid

*Thousand Island Dressing*
¼ cup light mayonnaise
¼ cup no-sugar-added ketchup (like Heinz Simply Ketchup)
3 tablespoons pickles, minced
1 tablespoon pickle juice
A dash of garlic powder
Salt and pepper to season

## DIRECTIONS

**REUBEN POCKETS:** Preheat oven to 375°F and coat a large rimmed baking sheet with cooking spray. Divide the pizza dough into 6 even small balls. Roll out each ball with a rolling pin into a rectangle shape, about 5x6 inches. Use a little flour to dust the counter to prevent sticking if needed. Repeat this with all 6 dough balls so there are 6 rectangles. Lay the slices of pastrami on one side of each rectangle, distributing evenly among the 6 pieces of dough. All of the filling will be layered on this side. Next, layer the Swiss cheese slices on the meat and top with a scoop of sauerkraut. Gently fold the bare portion of the dough over the filling to create a pocket. Seal the pocket with your fingers the entire way around. Transfer the pockets to the prepared baking sheet. Make sure there is at least 1 inch of space between pockets. Bake for 20 minutes or until the pockets are golden brown on the top and bottom.

**THOUSAND ISLAND DRESSING:** While the pockets bake, prepare the dressing. In a small bowl, whisk together light mayonnaise, ketchup, minced pickles, pickle juice, garlic powder, salt, and pepper until well combined. Serve the dressing with the pockets when they are finished baking.

# SEAFOOD & VEGETARIAN ENTREES

SPEEDY SUGAR-AND-SPICE SALMON

GRILLED SWORDFISH

GREEK SALMON

SOUTHWESTERN TILAPIA *WITH MANGO PEACH SALSA*

TUNA MELTS *WITH SHARP CHEDDAR*

CRAB CAKES *WITH BY-THE-BAY OVEN FRIES*

MEDITERRANEAN SHRIMP PASTA

SHRIMP PAD THAI

*PAN BAGNAT*—FRENCH TUNA SALAD NIÇOISE

COLORFUL CAULIFLOWER CURRY

MEATLESS MONDAY MEXI-CALI WRAPS *WITH MANGO SALAD*

CAULIFLOWER MACARONI AND CHEESE

LAUREN K'S PERFECT PIZZA

TINY PASTA *WITH FIRE ROASTED TOMATO SAUCE AND WILTED SPINACH*

# SPEEDY SUGAR-AND-SPICE SALMON

According to my brother Ian, and plenty of other people who have tried this dish, this is the most amazing salmon dish ever created. Plus, it's very simple to make! Fresh salmon works best in this recipe, but you can use frozen filets as well.

**PREP TIME:** 5 minutes     **BAKE TIME:** 20 minutes
**SERVINGS:** 4 filets
**TOTAL COST:** $12.83

## NUTRITIONAL INFORMATION

Calories: 285                Sodium: 301mg              Sugar: 4.6g
Total Fat: 14.2g             Carbohydrates: 4.6g        Protein: 33.8g
Saturated Fat: 2.1g          Fiber: 0g                  Cholesterol: 94mg

## INGREDIENTS

4  6-ounce salmon filets, fully thawed if frozen     1 tablespoon brown sugar, packed
Salt and pepper to season                            ½ teaspoon seafood seasoning, such as
1 tablespoon olive oil                               Old Bay

## DIRECTIONS

Preheat oven to 375°F. Spray a rimmed baking sheet with cooking spray. Lay out salmon filets on the baking sheet and season with salt and pepper. In a small bowl, mix the olive oil, brown sugar, and seafood seasoning together. The mixture will be grainy, but runny. With your fingers, spread the mixture evenly over the tops of the salmon filets. Bake until cooked through, about 20 minutes and serve with your favorite side dish.

## CHANGE IT UP!

**HONEY LIME SALMON:** Marinade salmon filets in a dressing of 1 tablespoon honey, 1 teaspoon chili powder, and the juice of 1 lime for 20 minutes. Bake at 375°F for 20 minutes.

## PERFECT PAIRINGS:

1. Roasted Potatoes: Cube 4 large yellow potatoes, toss with 1 tablespoon of olive oil and season with salt and pepper. Roast at 375°F for 30 minutes, turning once halfway through baking.

2. Easy Asparagus with Garlic and Parmesan (see p. 184)

3. Strawberry Spinach Salad with Creamy Poppy Seed Dressing  (see p. 96)

# GRILLED SWORDFISH

I call swordfish the "steak of the sea." This meaty fish tastes best when grilled. A simple lemon and herb marinade infuses flavors into the fish before cooking, and the grill adds the rest! Fresh swordfish can sometimes be expensive at the store, but it does show up on the sale flyer frequently for about $8.99 per pound for frozen whole steaks.

**PREP TIME:** 10 minutes    **COOK TIME:** 8–10 minutes
**SERVINGS:** 6 steaks
*TOTAL COST:* $16.22

## NUTRITIONAL INFORMATION

Calories: 200

Sodium: 227.6mg

Sugar: 0.2g

Total Fat: 8.1g

Carbohydrates: 1.1g

Protein: 28.9g

Saturated Fat: 1.9g

Fiber: 0.1g

Cholesterol: 56.7mg

## INGREDIENTS

1 tablespoon olive oil

Juice of 1 lemon

1 tablespoon fresh rosemary, chopped

1 tablespoon fresh thyme, chopped

2 cloves garlic, minced

1 ½ pounds swordfish steaks, fully thawed if frozen, cut into 6 portions

Salt and pepper to season

### PERFECT PAIRING

**Caprese Salad:** Place the following ingredients in a serving bowl and toss gently to combine:

8 ounces mini mozzarella balls
1 pint cherry tomatoes, halved
1 avocado, cubed
¼ cup fresh basil leaves, chopped
2 tablespoons balsamic vinegar
1 tablespoon olive oil

## DIRECTIONS

In a small bowl, combine the olive oil, lemon juice, rosemary, thyme, and garlic. This will be the marinade. Lay out swordfish filets in a shallow dish. Season the first side with salt and pepper. Spread half of the marinade mixture on one side of the swordfish steaks. Flip and repeat on the other side. Let the steaks marinade for at least 15 minutes, but no longer than 30 minutes.

Preheat grill pan or grill to medium heat. Grill the marinated steaks for 4–5 minutes per side. The steaks are done when they are firm to the touch. Remove from the grill and serve with your favorite side dish, such as corn on the cob or sautéed green beans.

# GREEK SALMON

Greek cuisine is one of my favorites! A few years ago, I created this recipe for a Greek-themed dinner party. I used fresh salmon I found on sale at the grocery store and some basic ingredients from my pantry and refrigerator.

**PREP TIME:** 15 minutes   **BAKE TIME:** 20 minutes
**SERVINGS:** 6 filets
**TOTAL COST:** $16.25 (using fresh salmon)

### PERFECT PAIRING

**Nutty Couscous:** Follow the package directions for 6 servings of boxed couscous, such as Near East, using chicken broth instead of water. Stir ⅓ cup fresh chopped parsley and ⅓ cup toasted pine nuts into the cooked couscous.

## NUTRITIONAL INFORMATION

Calories: 230
Total Fat: 9.9g
Saturated Fat: 1.9g

Sodium: 389mg
Carbohydrates: 7.7g
Fiber: 1.2g

Sugar: 1.6g
Protein: 25.9g
Cholesterol: 65.3mg

## INGREDIENTS

6  4-ounce salmon filets, fully thawed if frozen
Salt and pepper to season
14-ounce can artichoke hearts or quarters, drained and squeezed of liquid
1 clove garlic, minced

2 tablespoons light mayonnaise
¼ cup plain Greek yogurt
¼ cup parmesan cheese, grated
¼ cup breadcrumbs (any style)
Juice of ½ lemon

## DIRECTIONS

Preheat oven to 375°F and line a rimmed baking pan with foil. Grease with cooking spray to prevent sticking. Place salmon filets on the pan and season with salt and pepper.

For the topping, chop the artichokes, discarding any tough pieces that won't cut easily with a knife. Add artichokes, garlic, light mayonnaise, Greek yogurt, parmesan cheese, breadcrumbs, and lemon juice in a medium-sized bowl. Mix until well combined. Distribute the mixture evenly over each piece of salmon. Bake until cooked through, about 20 minutes. Remove from oven and serve hot.

# SOUTHWESTERN TILAPIA
## WITH MANGO PEACH SALSA

Tilapia is one of my favorite types of fish because its mild taste appeals to many palates. Spices such as chili powder, paprika, dried parsley, and garlic powder are typical pantry ingredients that come together to flavor your fish without adding a fatty sauce. Top this delicious fish with a fresh homemade mango peach salsa when peaches are fresh in the summertime. The serrano peppers, which are a mini version of a jalapeño, give it a perfect kick of heat.

**PREP TIME:** 20 minutes
**BAKE TIME:** 16–18 minutes
**SERVINGS:** 4, each with 1 4-ounce tilapia filet and ¾ cup salsa
**TOTAL COST:** $8.63

### NUTRITIONAL INFORMATION

Calories: 230
Total Fat: 4.4g
Saturated Fat: 1.2g

Sodium: 283.5mg
Carbohydrates: 20g
Fiber: 2.2g

Sugar: 16.5g
Protein: 30.4g
Cholesterol: 65.1mg

### INGREDIENTS
**Southwestern Tilapia**
1 pound fresh or frozen tilapia filets, fully thawed if frozen
½ teaspoon chili powder
½ teaspoon paprika
¼ teaspoon garlic powder
¼ teaspoon dried parsley
⅛ teaspoon salt
⅛ teaspoon pepper

*Mango Peach Salsa*

1 ripe mango, peeled and diced

2 medium peaches, diced

2 green onions, finely chopped

2 serrano peppers, seeds, stem, and ribbing removed and finely minced

½ teaspoon chili powder

2 teaspoons honey

1 teaspoon olive oil

Juice of 1 lime

⅛ teaspoon salt

---

## DIRECTIONS

**SOUTHWESTERN TILAPIA:** Preheat oven to 375°F and line a rimmed baking sheet with foil. Spray with cooking spray to prevent sticking. Lay out tilapia filets on the foil. In a small bowl, mix together chili powder, paprika, garlic powder, dried parsley, salt, and pepper. Season both sides of the tilapia filets with the spice mix. Bake for 16–18 minutes or until the fish is opaque in color and flakes away easily with a fork.

**MANGO PEACH SALSA:** In a medium mixing bowl, combine the mango, peaches, green onions, serrano peppers, chili powder, honey, olive oil, lime juice, and salt. Gently fold to combine. Serve on top of the tilapia filets.

# TUNA MELTS
## *WITH SHARP CHEDDAR*

Tuna is one of the most cost-effective ways to pump up the protein in your diet. I never cared for canned tuna until my husband made me this tuna melt one day—it was delicious! When you add a variety of ingredients to canned tuna, it takes on a whole new flavor profile, just like in these yummy hot sandwiches that are fit for lunch or dinner.

**TOTAL TIME:** 20 minutes
**SERVINGS:** 5 melts
*TOTAL COST:* $7.51

### NUTRITIONAL INFORMATION

Calories: 241

Total Fat: 8.9g

Saturated Fat: 2.7g

Sodium: 766mg

Carbohydrates: 23.2g

Fiber: 5.2g

Sugar: 2.2g

Protein: 21.2g

Cholesterol: 73.2mg

### INGREDIENTS

3 5-ounce cans chunk light tuna, well drained

¼ cup green onions, finely chopped

1 clove garlic, minced

1 egg

3 tablespoons pickles, finely chopped (about 3 mini pickles)

1 teaspoon Dijon or yellow mustard

2 teaspoons hot sauce, such as Red Hot

Salt and pepper to season

1 tablespoon olive oil

½ cup grated sharp cheddar cheese or 5 thin slices of sharp cheddar

5 whole wheat sandwich thins or English muffins

### DIRECTIONS

**Serve with some fresh raw veggies for the perfect simple plate.**

Combine the tuna, green onion, garlic, egg, pickles, mustard, hot sauce, and a pinch of salt and pepper in a medium mixing bowl. Mix thoroughly and form into 5 patties. Heat 1 tablespoon of olive oil in a large skillet over medium heat. Gently lay the patties onto the skillet and cook for 3–4 minutes on the first side. Gently flip over the patties and then top the cooked side with the sharp cheddar cheese. Cook for an additional 3 minutes or until the cheese is fully melted. Lay the melts on the sandwich thins and serve hot.

# CRAB CAKES
## *WITH BY-THE-BAY OVEN FRIES*

When it comes to crab meat, I purchase it only when it's on sale for about $12.99 per pound or less. You can find good canned crab meat refrigerated in the seafood section in 1-pound cans. Use 12 ounces of crab for this dish and 4 ounces for another dish! This made-over recipe was inspired by Paula Deen's famous crab cakes recipe.

**TOTAL TIME:** 35 minutes
**SERVINGS:** 4, each with 2 crab cakes and 1 cup of oven fries
*TOTAL COST:* $13.56

### NUTRITIONAL INFORMATION

| | | |
|---|---|---|
| Calories: 402 | Sodium: 832.7mg | Sugar: 4g |
| Total Fat: 15.5g | Carbohydrates: 48.6g | Protein: 17.3g |
| Saturated Fat: 2.4g | Fiber: 5.1g | Cholesterol: 90.9mg |

### INGREDIENTS

*Fries*
4 medium baking potatoes, like Russet
    or Idaho
1 tablespoon olive oil, divided
1–2 teaspoons Old Bay Seasoning
Salt and pepper to season

**This meal is packed full of vitamins and nutrients, especially Vitamin B and C!**

*Crab Cakes*
12 ounces lump crab meat (about 1 ½ cups)
1 egg
½ cup Italian seasoned breadcrumbs
½ red bell pepper, finely chopped
1 teaspoon hot sauce
1 tablespoon Dijon mustard
1 tablespoon light mayonnaise
4 green onions, chopped
Salt and pepper to season
2 tablespoons olive oil

### DIRECTIONS

**FRIES:** Preheat oven to 400°F. Line a rimmed baking sheet with foil and spray with cooking spray to prevent sticking. Wash and scrub potatoes, and cut into fry-sized pieces. Lay the potatoes out on the baking sheet. Toss with 1 tablespoon of the olive oil, the Old Bay seasoning, and salt and pepper. Spread out on the baking sheet into an even layer. Bake for 30 minutes or until tender.

**CRAB CAKES:** Meanwhile, in a medium mixing bowl, combine the crab meat, egg, breadcrumbs, red bell pepper, hot sauce, Dijon mustard, mayonnaise, green onions, and a pinch of salt and pepper. Mix thoroughly to combine. Shape crab mixture into 8 cakes. Heat the remaining 2 tablespoons of olive oil in a large skillet over medium heat. Gently lay the crab cakes into the oil and cook for 4–5 minutes per side or until golden brown on each side. Serve with the fries.

# MEDITERRANEAN SHRIMP PASTA

This crowd-pleasing pasta dish integrates all of the flavors I love about Greek and Italian dining. By creating a sauce with white wine and chicken broth and using fresh herbs, vegetables, and flavorful feta cheese, this dish gives you a satisfying big plate of shrimp pasta and leaves the fat and calories behind.

**Look for shrimp on sale for around $8 per pound for the best deal.**

**TOTAL TIME:** 40 minutes
**SERVINGS:** 6, about 2 cups each
*TOTAL COST:* $18.54

## NUTRITIONAL INFORMATION

Calories: 460
Total Fat: 12.5g
Saturated Fat: 2.4g

Sodium: 697mg
Carbohydrates: 63.9g
Fiber: 8.9g

Sugar: 3g
Protein: 25.8g
Cholesterol: 126.4mg

## INGREDIENTS

13.25 ounces whole wheat penne pasta
1 tablespoon olive oil
1 medium onion, diced
3 garlic cloves, minced
16 ounces large raw shrimp, thawed, peeled, deveined, and tails removed

Salt and pepper to season
2 tablespoons flour
½ cup chicken broth
½ cup white wine
14-ounce can of artichoke hearts, drained, squeezed of liquid, and roughly chopped

½ cup Kalamata olives, roughly chopped
1 pint grape or cherry tomatoes, halved
½ cup feta cheese, crumbled
¼ cup fresh parsley, chopped
¼ cup green onions, chopped
Juice of 1 lemon

## DIRECTIONS

Fill a large stock pot with water and bring to a boil. Meanwhile, prepare the onions, garlic, artichokes, olives, tomatoes, parsley, and green onions so they are ready to use in the recipe quickly. Once the water comes to a boil, salt the water and cook the pasta according to package directions. Drain, but do not rinse.

In a large sauté skillet, heat 1 tablespoon of olive oil over medium heat. Add onions and garlic and sauté for about 3 minutes, stirring often. Add the shrimp to the pan, season with salt and pepper, and cook until just pink, about 2 minutes. Do not overcook. Sprinkle the flour over the shrimp mixture and stir to coat evenly. Cook for 1 minute and then add the chicken broth and white wine to deglaze the pan and create a sauce. Stir this mixture constantly for about 1 minute and then add the artichokes, olives, tomatoes, and cooked pasta. Cook until heated through, about 2 minutes. Remove from heat and top with feta cheese, parsley, green onions, and lemon juice. Toss gently and season with salt and pepper if needed. Serve hot with your favorite side salad.

# SHRIMP PAD THAI

My first taste of true Thai cuisine was Pad Thai, a sweet but savory rice noodle dish. I've ordered it dozens of times, but I like to make it at home when I can't get to a Thai restaurant in the city. You can add whatever protein you like, but shrimp is my personal favorite. The ingredients below will make the mild version of this dish, but you can increase the amount of red pepper flakes or add chili peppers for an extra kick!

**TOTAL TIME:** 40 minutes
**SERVINGS:** 4, about 1 ½ cups each
**TOTAL COST:** $14.89

## NUTRITIONAL INFORMATION

| | | |
|---|---|---|
| Calories: 477 | Sodium: 793.3mg | Sugar: 14g |
| Total Fat: 12.4g | Carbohydrates: 66.4g | Protein: 26.8g |
| Saturated Fat: 2.2g | Fiber: 4.4g | Cholesterol: 222.2mg |

## INGREDIENTS

**Pad Thai Sauce**
1 tablespoon fish sauce
2 tablespoons brown sugar
2 tablespoons ketchup
1 tablespoon rice vinegar
Juice of ½ lime

**Pad Thai Noodle Mixture**
7 ounces rice noodles, uncooked
1 tablespoon olive oil
4 cloves garlic, minced
1 medium onion, sliced
12 ounces large raw shrimp, thawed, peeled, deveined, and tails removed
¼ teaspoon red pepper flakes
Salt and pepper to season
14.5-ounce can bean sprouts, drained
2 eggs, lightly beaten
¼ cup green onions, chopped
¼ cup parsley, chopped
¼ cup peanuts, chopped

## DIRECTIONS

To prepare the Pad Thai sauce, whisk together the fish sauce, brown sugar, ketchup, rice vinegar, and lime juice. Set aside.

Bring a large pot of water to a boil. Follow the package directions for preparing the rice noodles. Meanwhile, chop, prepare, and clean the remaining ingredients.

In a large sauté pan, heat 1 tablespoon of olive oil over medium heat. Add the garlic and onions and cook for 3 minutes to soften. Add the shrimp and red pepper flakes, and season with salt and pepper. Cook just until the shrimp are pink, about 2–3 minutes. Remove the mixture from the pan into a separate bowl. Cover the bowl with foil to keep warm. Return pan to burner. Add the bean sprouts to one side of the pan. Stir to heat for 2 minutes. On the other side of the pan, add the beaten eggs and season lightly with salt and pepper. Stir gently until no longer runny, about 2 minutes, and then stir the eggs together with the hot bean sprouts. Once the eggs are cooked and the bean sprouts are hot, add the rice noodles and Pad Thai sauce. Gently toss to combine. Add the shrimp mixture, green onions, parsley, and peanuts to the pan and toss to coat again. Serve hot.

# PAN BAGNAT—
## *FRENCH TUNA SALAD NIÇOISE*

When I took my track and field competitors to the state championships one year, we stayed in historic Gettysburg. One night, we visited Café St. Amand, a bistro that serves the most delicious classic French food, including an amazing Niçoise-style tuna sandwich. With this recipe, you can bring France to your table for under $6!

**TOTAL TIME:** 15 minutes
**SERVINGS:** 4, 2 open-faced sandwiches each
***TOTAL COST:*** $5.99

### NUTRITIONAL INFORMATION

Calories: 210
Total Fat: 8.6g
Saturated Fat: 0.5g

Sodium: 632mg
Carbohydrates: 18.5g
Fiber: 1g

Sugar: 0.4g
Protein: 13.2g
Cholesterol: 25mg

### INGREDIENTS

2 5-ounce cans solid white albacore tuna, drained
½ cup red bell pepper, finely chopped (about ¼ of a pepper)
¼ cup Kalamata olives, chopped
2 tablespoons parsley, chopped

2 tablespoons red wine vinegar
1 tablespoon extra virgin olive oil
Half of a French baguette, sliced on the bias (8 slices), OR 4 whole wheat pita pockets, halved

**Though slightly more expensive, solid white albacore tuna tastes more like chicken than chunk tuna, so it appeals to more palates.**

### DIRECTIONS

Combine the tuna, red bell pepper, Kalamata olives, parsley, red wine vinegar, and extra virgin olive oil in a bowl. Use a spoon to mix well. Top bread slices with the tuna salad and serve.

# COLORFUL CAULIFLOWER CURRY

When I lived in Pittsburgh, I was introduced to a variety of cultures and cuisines; Indian curry became one of my favorite dinner staples. This dish features a creamy curry sauce that has intense flavor and lots of great healthy ingredients. You will love it!

**TOTAL TIME:** 30 minutes

**SERVINGS:** 4

*TOTAL COST:* $9.75

**NUTRITIONAL INFORMATION** (using roasted chicken for the protein)

| | | |
|---|---|---|
| Calories: 231 | Sodium: 240mg | Sugar: 2.6g |
| Total Fat: 4.9g | Carbohydrates: 16.1g | Protein: 31.7g |
| Saturated Fat: 1.9g | Fiber: 5.3g | Cholesterol: 75.9mg |

## INGREDIENTS

1 tablespoon olive oil

3 cloves garlic, minced

1 large onion, sliced

1 orange, yellow, or red bell pepper, chopped

½ large head of cauliflower, cut into small florets (about 5 cups)

Salt and pepper to season

1 pound or 2 cups of your favorite fully cooked protein

1 tablespoon flour

½ cup chicken or vegetable broth

¼ cup plain Greek yogurt

¼ cup light sour cream

2 teaspoons curry powder

1 teaspoon paprika, preferably smoked or Hungarian

2 tablespoons fresh parsley, chopped

3 green onions, roughly chopped

## DIRECTIONS

In a large skillet, heat 1 tablespoon of olive oil over medium heat. Add the garlic, onion, bell peppers, and cauliflower florets to the pan and cook for about 5 minutes or until the vegetables begin to soften. Add your cooked protein choice and heat for an additional 2 minutes. Sprinkle 1 tablespoon of flour over the meat and veggie mixture and cook for another minute.

In a separate small bowl, combine the chicken or vegetable broth, Greek yogurt, light sour cream, curry powder, and paprika. Whisk together and then add to the skillet with the meat and vegetables. Cook until the sauce begins to thicken and the mixture is simmering, about 2–3 minutes. Remove from the heat and sprinkle in chopped parsley and green onions. Serve hot.

## YOU CAN USE ANY COOKED PROTEIN IN THIS DISH. HERE ARE SOME AFFORDABLE OPTIONS:

- 1 pound boneless skinless chicken breast or thighs

- 1 pound turkey sausage

- 12 ounces shrimp

- 15 ounces chickpeas, drained and rinsed

- 16 ounces extra firm tofu, drained and cubed

- 1 pound cubed sirloin steak

# MEATLESS MONDAY
# MEXI-CALI WRAPS
## *WITH MANGO SALAD*

The "Meatless Mondays" trend is the best friend of budget-friendly, healthy meals. Southwestern ingredients—such as black beans, avocado, mango, and lime—flavor this vegetarian dish beautifully. This meal is *very* filling, so you won't be leaving the dinner table hungry!

**BAKE TIME:** 20 minutes    **TOTAL TIME:** 30 minutes
**SERVINGS:** 5, 1 wrap and 1 cup of salad each
*TOTAL COST:* $10.88

## NUTRITIONAL INFORMATION

| | | |
|---|---|---|
| Calories: 440 | Sodium: 455mg | Sugar: 14.4g |
| Total Fat: 11.8g | Carbohydrates: 75.9g | Protein: 13.2g |
| Saturated Fat: 2.4g | Fiber: 12.6g | Cholesterol: 2mg |

## INGREDIENTS
### Mexi-Cali Wraps
2 medium sweet potatoes, sliced evenly into fry-sized pieces
15-ounce can black beans, drained and thoroughly rinsed
1 cup fresh or frozen corn
¼ cup green onions, chopped
¼ cup fresh parsley OR cilantro, chopped
1 avocado, cut into small cubes (half for the wraps and half for the salad*)
2 tablespoons plain low-fat Greek yogurt
2 tablespoons light sour cream
1 lime, juiced (half for the wraps and half for the salad*)
Salt and pepper to season
5 whole wheat 10-inch tortillas (150 calories or less each)

*Mango Salad*

1 ripe mango, peeled and cubed

5 cups mixed greens (about a 5-ounce bag)

*½ avocado, cubed, reserved from wraps

*Juice of ½ lime, reserved from wraps

1 tablespoon honey

1 tablespoon extra virgin olive oil

1 tablespoon apple cider vinegar

Salt and pepper to season

---

## DIRECTIONS

**MEXI-CALI WRAPS:** Preheat oven to 400°F. Spray a rimmed baking sheet generously with cooking spray. Spritz the sweet potato pieces with cooking spray and season with salt and pepper. Toss to coat and bake for 20 minutes or until a fork can pierce the pieces easily.

Meanwhile, place the rinsed black beans, corn, green onions, and parsley (or cilantro) in a large mixing bowl. When the sweet potatoes are finished cooking, let them cool for 5 minutes and then add them to the bean mixture. In a separate small bowl, combine half of the avocado, Greek yogurt, light sour cream, juice of ½ lime, and a pinch of salt and pepper. Mash the mixture with a fork to form a thick dressing. Add to the sweet potato/black bean mixture and fold gently to coat. Spoon the filling in the center of the 5 wraps, distributing evenly in the shape of a rectangle. For each wrap, fold one side over the filling, fold in the sides, and roll the wrap to close. Cut in half for serving if desired.

**MANGO SALAD:** Combine the mango, mixed greens, and remaining avocado cubes in a medium serving bowl. In a separate small bowl, whisk together the juice of the remaining half of a lime, honey, olive oil, apple cider vinegar, and a pinch of salt and pepper. Drizzle over the mango salad, toss to coat, and serve with the wraps.

# CAULIFLOWER MACARONI AND CHEESE

There is no one in the world that eats as much macaroni and cheese as my best friend Erin. People actually brought boxes of Velveeta Shells and Easy Mac as gifts to her wedding. When my sister-in-law Shannon said I should try to make a healthy macaroni recipe for Erin, cauliflower immediately came to mind as my secret ingredient. This dish also features two flavor-punching cheeses—sharp cheddar and Asiago—so you can use less cheese *and* cut out heavy ingredients like heavy cream and butter without sacrificing flavor. Enjoy!

**PREP TIME:** 25 minutes    **BAKE TIME:** 20–25 minutes
**SERVINGS:** 8, 1 cup each
*TOTAL COST:* $9.86

## NUTRITIONAL INFORMATION

Calories: 346

Total Fat: 17.7g

Saturated Fat: 10.3g

Sodium: 386mg

Carbohydrates: 29.1g

Fiber: 3.2g

Sugar: 2.8g

Protein: 18.3g

Cholesterol: 50mg

## INGREDIENTS

8 ounces whole wheat mini pasta shells or macaroni

6 cups cauliflower florets

2 tablespoons butter

2 tablespoons flour

1 ½ cups low-fat milk

1 teaspoon Worcestershire sauce

½ teaspoon paprika

8 ounces sharp cheddar, freshly grated

4 ounces Asiago cheese, freshly grated

Salt and pepper to season

## DIRECTIONS

Preheat oven to 350°F and spray a 4-quart baking dish with cooking spray. Bring a large stock pot half full of water to a boil. Salt the water, add pasta shells, and cook for 2 minutes. Add cauliflower florets and cook for another 4 minutes. Drain pasta and cauliflower into a strainer. The pasta will not be fully cooked—it will finish cooking in the oven.

In the stock pot, melt 2 tablespoons of butter over medium heat. Sprinkle the flour around the pan and whisk the flour into the butter to create a roux. Cook for about 30 seconds, whisking constantly. Vigorously whisk in the milk and bring mixture to a simmer. The sauce should begin to thicken. Add in the Worcestershire sauce, paprika, sharp cheddar cheese, and Asiago cheese. Season with salt and pepper. Whisk vigorously again until a smooth cheese sauce forms and then immediately remove from heat. Pour the cauliflower and pasta into the cheese sauce and fold until the cheese sauce is evenly dispersed. Pour the macaroni and cheese into the baking dish and bake for 20–25 minutes or until the mixture is bubbly. Remove from the oven and serve hot.

# LAUREN K'S PERFECT PIZZA

Pay tribute to this Italian-American classic by making your own pizza at home for under $5! I usually build pizzas on rectangular baking sheets to yield more total pieces of pizza. Feel free to add your own toppings, such as sausage, pepperoni, green peppers, mushrooms, or onions.

**PREP TIME:** 10 minutes
**BAKE TIME:** 18–20 minutes
**SERVINGS:** 6, 2 slices each
**TOTAL COST:** $4.70

## NUTRITIONAL INFORMATION

Calories: 297
Total Fat: 9.3g
Saturated Fat: 4.8g

Sodium: 847.7mg
Carbohydrates: 38.7g
Fiber: 2.4g

Sugar: 5.3g
Protein: 15.8g
Cholesterol: 25.3mg

## INGREDIENTS

1 pound whole wheat pizza dough (see p. 84 to make your own)
1 cup spaghetti or pizza sauce (under 50 calories per serving)
1 ½ cups Italian blend cheese, grated
½ cup parmesan cheese, grated
1 ½ teaspoons dried Italian herbs, such as basil, parsley, and/or oregano
Salt and pepper to season

## DIRECTIONS

Preheat oven to 400°F. Grease a large rectangular rimmed baking sheet with cooking spray. Roll out the pizza dough with a rolling pin to fit the size of the pan. Lay the dough on the pan and top with the spaghetti or pizza sauce. Top with the cheeses and Italian seasoning, and lightly season with salt and pepper. Bake for 18–20 minutes or until cheese is bubbling and beginning to brown. Cut into 12 squares and serve hot.

# TINY PASTA
## *WITH FIRE ROASTED TOMATO SAUCE AND WILTED SPINACH*

Looking for an easy supper that can be ready to eat in less than fifteen minutes? This delicious pasta dish will please your wallet, waistline, and palate all at the same time.

**TOTAL TIME:** 12 minutes
**SERVINGS:** 4, 1 ¼ cup each
*TOTAL COST:* $7.72

### NUTRITIONAL INFORMATION

Calories: 316

Total Fat: 5.2g

Saturated Fat: 0.5g

Sodium: 406.7mg

Carbohydrates: 55.2g

Fiber: 6.7g

Sugar: 9.3g

Protein: 9.2g

Cholesterol: 0mg

### INGREDIENTS

8 ounces small, short cut whole wheat pasta, such as orzo, couscous or orecchiette

1 tablespoon olive oil

3 garlic cloves, minced

2 15 ounce cans fire roasted diced tomatoes

¼ teaspoon fresh cracked black pepper

10 ounces fresh spinach

### WANT TO ADD SOME PROTEIN?

Add one of the following to your meal to keep you full and satisfied.

- 12 ounces roasted chicken breast

- 8 ounces cooked and crumbled turkey sausage

- 8 ounces cooked lean beef or turkey meatballs

- ¾ cup parmesan or Italian blend cheese

### DIRECTIONS

Cook pasta according to package directions. In a large skillet, heat the olive oil over medium heat. Sauté the garlic for 1 minute. Add in the fire roasted tomatoes and bring to a simmer. Stir in the spinach and cook until wilted. Serve the tomato sauce over the pasta and enjoy hot.

# SIDE DISHES

EASY ASPARAGUS WITH GARLIC AND PARMESAN

CRUNCHY BROCCOLI

BUTTERNUT SQUASH FRIES

CAULI-TATOES

ROASTED CABBAGE OR CAULIFLOWER STEAKS

ROASTED SWEET POTATOES WITH APPLES AND PEARS

STUFFED TOMATOES

TWICE-BAKED SWEET POTATOES

YELLOW SQUASH CASSEROLE

# EASY ASPARAGUS
## WITH GARLIC AND PARMESAN

This is an impressive side dish that, with little effort and cost, will wow your guests. Asparagus is a delicious way to get green veggies packed full of vitamins and nutrients into your family's diet. Look for asparagus on sale for $2.99 per pound or less for the best buy.

**PREP TIME:** 8 minutes  **BAKE TIME:** 10–15 minutes
**SERVINGS:** 4
**TOTAL COST:** $3.62

### NUTRITIONAL INFORMATION

Calories: 71

Total Fat: 4.4g

Saturated Fat: 1.0g

Sodium: 165.5mg

Carbohydrates: 6.0g

Fiber: 2.4g

Sugar: 0.0g

Protein: 3.8g

Cholesterol: 2mg

### INGREDIENTS

1 pound fresh asparagus

1 tablespoon olive oil

⅛ teaspoon salt

⅛ teaspoon black pepper

3 cloves garlic, minced

2 tablespoons grated parmesan cheese

To buy fresh asparagus with the best taste and texture, select thin, bright green stalks over thick, browning stalks.

### DIRECTIONS

Preheat oven to 375°F. Line a baking sheet with foil and coat with a thin layer of cooking spray. Keeping the asparagus bundled with the rubber bands, use a chef's knife to trim about 1 inch off the bottom ends of the asparagus, all at the same time. Spread asparagus in an even layer on the baking sheet. Drizzle the olive oil and sprinkle salt and black pepper over the asparagus and toss to coat. Sprinkle half of garlic and parmesan over the asparagus. Toss again. Sprinkle the remaining garlic and parmesan cheese evenly over the top of asparagus. Bake for 10–15 minutes or until tender but still crispy. Serve hot.

# CRUNCHY BROCCOLI

Of all vegetable dishes I demonstrate to my high school students, this one never fails to please. It's a super simple recipe that bakes while you get your main dish ready. The final product actually reminds me of popcorn! My dad likes to eat this instead of chips for an evening snack.

**PREP TIME:** 5 minutes    **BAKE TIME:** 30–40 minutes
**SERVINGS:** 4 (or eat the whole thing by yourself for about 280 calories!)
*TOTAL COST:* $3.25

## NUTRITIONAL INFORMATION

Calories: 70                    Sodium: 186.6mg                Sugar: 0.2g
Total Fat: 3.9g                Carbohydrates: 7.6g            Protein: 4.1g
Saturated Fat: 0.5g        Fiber: 4.1g                          Cholesterol: 0mg

## INGREDIENTS

1 large or 2 medium heads fresh broccoli, cut into florets
1 tablespoon olive oil
Salt and black pepper (about ¼ teaspoon each)
1 teaspoon garlic powder

## DIRECTIONS

Preheat oven to 400°F. Coat a rimmed baking sheet with cooking spray. Lay the florets out in an even layer and drizzle with olive oil. Season with salt, pepper, and garlic powder. Toss to coat evenly. Bake for 30 minutes for softer broccoli or 35–40 for crispier broccoli. It will become browned and slightly charred. Sprinkle with a few dashes of salt before serving, if desired.

# BUTTERNUT SQUASH FRIES

Every sandwich pairs well with fries, but I like to get as many colorful veggies into my diet as possible. This dish looks and tastes like a softer version of a sweet potato fry. Kids and adults alike love this dippable finger food!

**PREP TIME:** 15 minutes
**BAKE TIME:** 18–20 minutes
**SERVINGS:** 4
**TOTAL COST:** $3.15

## NUTRITIONAL INFORMATION

| | | |
|---|---|---|
| Calories: 148 | Sodium: 273.3mg | Sugar: 1.5g |
| Total Fat: 3.7g | Carbohydrates: 31.3g | Protein: 2.5g |
| Saturated Fat: 0.5g | Fiber:8.3g | Cholesterol: 0mg |

### PREP TIP: HOW TO PEEL AND SLICE A BUTTERNUT SQUASH

Peel the skin off the squash with a good peeler. With a sturdy chef's knife, trim off each end of the squash. Cut the squash in half to separate the top and bottom. Then, cut the bottom in half lengthwise. Using a soup spoon, scrape out and discard the seeds. Cut the remaining hard flesh into desired shapes.

### INGREDIENTS
1 medium butternut squash
   (about 2 ½ pounds)
1 tablespoon olive oil
Salt and pepper to season
1 teaspoon brown sugar
½ teaspoon Old Bay seasoning
See my optional dip ideas!

## DIRECTIONS

Preheat oven to 400°F. Line a jellyroll pan with foil and coat with cooking spray to prevent sticking. Peel and slice the squash into fry-sized slices. Be sure to cut them into similar-sized pieces to ensure even baking. Spread fries into an even layer on the baking sheet. Drizzle with olive oil and sprinkle with salt, pepper, brown sugar, and Old Bay seasoning. Toss to coat completely. Bake the fries for about 18–20 minutes or until a fork can pierce the fries easily. Sprinkle with a little additional salt if desired and serve hot with BBQ sauce or ketchup.

### TIME-SAVING TIP

Get a big squash for this recipe (about 5 pounds) and cut the whole thing up. Store the unused portion in a plastic bag for use in another recipe later in the week, like Butternut Squash Salad with Caramelized Onions and Feta on page 95.

### 4 FUN DIPS FOR YOUR FRIES
### *FOR UNDER 50 CALORIES* PER TABLESPOON

- Sriracha Mayo: 4 tablespoons light mayonnaise plus 2 teaspoons Sriracha sauce

- Spicy Syrup: ¼ cup pure maple syrup with 2 teaspoons Old Bay seasoning

- Hot BBQ Sauce: ¼ cup BBQ sauce plus 2 teaspoons hot sauce or Sriracha sauce

- Lauren K Ketchup: 3 tablespoons no-sugar-added ketchup and 1 tablespoon brown sugar

# CAULI-TATOES

When it comes to side dish requests, my husband's first choice is always mashed potatoes. However, this heavy side dish tends to get a bad rap for being saturated with butter and heavy cream. With a few secret swaps, this recipe will wow your guests and leave you showered in compliments!

**TOTAL TIME:** 30 minutes
**SERVINGS:** 6, about 1 cup each
**TOTAL COST:** $3.79

## NUTRITIONAL INFORMATION

Calories: 215

Total Fat: 8.1g

Saturated Fat: 5.1g

Sodium: 283.5mg

Carbohydrates: 29.6g

Fiber:4.3g

Sugar: 2.8g

Protein: 7.9g

Cholesterol: 22.3mg

## INGREDIENTS

5 cups potatoes, cut into 1-inch cubes (about 4 large potatoes)

5 cups cauliflower, cut into florets (about ½ large head)

¼ cup low-fat milk

¼ cup light sour cream

¼ cup parmesan cheese

¼ cup cottage cheese

3 tablespoons butter, cut into small squares

Salt and pepper to season

## DIRECTIONS

Fill a stock pot with water and bring to a boil over high heat. Salt the water if desired. Add the cubed potatoes and cauliflower florets and boil for about 15 minutes. When the potatoes and cauliflower can be easily smashed on the side of the pot, they are done and can be drained in a colander. Add the potato-cauliflower mixture into the bowl of a stand mixer. Begin mashing the mixture on low speed for about 2 minutes. If you don't have a stand mixer, simply place your potatoes and cauliflower in a large bowl and use an electric hand mixer instead.

Next, mix the milk, sour cream, parmesan cheese, and cottage cheese in a small bowl. Once the potatoes and cauliflower start to mash and come together, add the milk mixture, cubed butter, salt, and pepper. Whip the cauli-tatoes until they are smooth. Season with additional salt and pepper if desired and serve hot.

## LAUREN'S LEFTOVER TIP: POTATO PANCAKES

Make some yummy potato pancakes by mixing leftover Cauli-tatoes with 3 chopped green onions, 1 egg, and 2 tablespoons flour. Shape them into palm-sized patties and fry in 1 tablespoon butter or olive oil for about 4 minutes per side over medium heat. These are equally delicious and are basically a freebie side-dish for tomorrow night's dinner.

# ROASTED CABBAGE OR CAULIFLOWER STEAKS

It doesn't get much easier and more delicious than this super simple and inexpensive side dish! These huge "steaks" are tasty whether you use cabbage or cauliflower. Pair with Mom and Dad's London Broil on page 154, Italian Chicken Cutlets on page 122, or turn the Baked Chicken Egg Roll appetizer on page 40 into a full dinner with this as a side.

**PREP TIME:** 8 minutes

**BAKE TIME:** 30–35 minutes

**SERVINGS:** 6 large steaks

**TOTAL COST:** $2.58

## NUTRITIONAL INFORMATION

Calories: 92

Total Fat: 5.1g

Saturated Fat: 0.7g

Sodium: 474.5mg

Carbohydrates: 11.4g

Fiber: 4.8g

Sugar: 0g

Protein:3g

Cholesterol: 0mg

## INGREDIENTS

1 large head cabbage or cauliflower

2 tablespoons olive oil

Salt and pepper to season

1 tablespoon Montreal Steak Seasoning, or one of my dry spice mixes

## DIRECTIONS

Preheat oven to 400°F. Line a large rimmed baking sheet with foil and spray with olive oil spray to prevent sticking. Cut out the bottom stem and core from the cabbage or cauliflower using a sharp paring knife. Pull off the older leaves from the outside if needed. Discard core, stem, and outside leaves. Start at one end of the head and cut the cabbage or cauliflower vertically into ½-inch thick rounds. Gently lay out the steaks on the pan in an even layer.

**SPICE UP YOUR DINNER WITH THESE DRY SPICE MIX OPTIONS:**

- 1 teaspoon curry powder plus 1 teaspoon garam masala

- 1 teaspoon chili powder plus 1 teaspoons paprika

- 1 teaspoon garlic powder plus 1 teaspoon dried Italian herbs

Use a basting brush to distribute the olive oil evenly over the entire top surface of the steaks. Season with salt and pepper. Sprinkle each with about ½ teaspoon of Montreal Steak Seasoning or desired spice mix. Press the spice mixture gently into the creases using the basting brush or your fingers. Bake for 30–35 minutes or until the steaks begin to brown slightly and can be cut easily with a knife. Serve immediately.

# ROASTED SWEET POTATOES
## WITH APPLES AND PEARS

I love scouring the farmers market for fresh, affordable fall fruits and vegetables to make seasonal dishes like this one. Golden Delicious and Honey Crisp apples are perfect for this side dish, but you can use whatever you have on hand.

**PREP TIME:** 15 minutes
**BAKE TIME:** 30 minutes
**SERVINGS:** 8, 1 cup each
*TOTAL COST:* $6.35

### NUTRITIONAL INFORMATION

Calories: 118

Total Fat: 2.5g

Saturated Fat: 0.3g

Sodium: 83.4mg

Carbohydrates: 26.2g

Fiber: 3.9g

Sugar: 18.7g

Protein: 0.8g

Cholesterol: 0mg

**Substitute butternut squash cubes for the potatoes for a less starchy side dish.**

### INGREDIENTS

1 large sweet potato, cut into 1-inch cubes (about 3 cups)

4 teaspoons olive oil, divided

2 tablespoons brown sugar, divided

2 teaspoons fresh sage (or 1 teaspoon dried), minced and divided

2 teaspoons fresh thyme (or 1 teaspoon dried), minced and divided

Salt and pepper to season

3 large apples, cored and cut into 1-inch cubes

2 large pears, cored and cut into 1-inch cubes

2 tablespoons good-quality balsamic vinegar, divided

## DIRECTIONS

Preheat oven to 375°F. Line a rimmed baking sheet with foil and spray with olive oil spray. Lay the sweet potato cubes on the pan in an even layer. Drizzle with 2 teaspoons olive oil and sprinkle 1 tablespoon brown sugar, 1 teaspoon fresh sage, and 1 teaspoon fresh thyme evenly over the potatoes. Season with salt and pepper and toss to coat evenly. Roast in the oven for about 20 minutes.

Place the apple and pear cubes in a mixing bowl, drizzle with 2 teaspoons olive oil, and sprinkle with the remaining 1 tablespoon brown sugar, 1 teaspoon fresh sage, and 1 teaspoon fresh thyme. Season the apples and pears with salt and pepper. Toss to coat evenly and dump onto the sweet potato baking sheet after the sweet potato cubes have cooked for 20 minutes. Roast the apple/pear/sweet potato mixture in the oven for about 10 more minutes. Remove from the oven and allow mixture to cool slightly.

Drizzle 1 tablespoon of balsamic vinegar over the roasted apples, pears, and sweet potatoes, and toss gently with a spatula. Transfer to a serving bowl and drizzle the remaining 1 tablespoon of balsamic vinegar over the top of the salad. Enjoy warm or at room temperature.

## LEFTOVER LUNCH

Serve leftovers over mixed greens. Top with grilled chicken, feta or blue cheese, and balsamic vinaigrette.

# STUFFED TOMATOES

Few things are better than a garden fresh tomato in the summer. My mom often makes this side dish when tomatoes are abundant in her garden. This simple, but delicious recipe can also serve as a meatless main entrée.

**PREP TIME:** 25 minutes
**BAKE TIME:** 60 minutes
**SERVINGS:** 8 tomatoes
*TOTAL COST:* $9.30

## NUTRITIONAL INFORMATION

Calories: 156
Total Fat: 6.8g
Saturated Fat: 0.8g

Sodium: 300mg
Carbohydrates: 23.5g
Fiber: 2.5g

Sugar: 0.1g
Protein: 2.9g
Cholesterol: 1.1mg

## INGREDIENTS

1 ¾ cup chicken or vegetable broth
2 cups dry instant brown rice
8 medium tomatoes
3 garlic cloves, minced
¼ cup fresh basil, chopped
¼ cup fresh parsley, chopped
¼ teaspoon salt
¼ teaspoon pepper
8 teaspoons olive oil, divided

> Tomatoes contain lycopene, an antioxidant that may reduce the risk of heart disease and certain types of cancer.

## DIRECTIONS

Preheat oven to 375°F. Spray a 13x9 baking pan with 2-inch sides with cooking spray. In a medium saucepan, bring the chicken or vegetable broth to a boil. Add rice and simmer, covered, for 5 minutes. Remove from heat and keep covered for 5 additional minutes.

As the rice cooks, wash and dry your tomatoes. Using a paring knife, core each tomato, reserving the tomato tops. With a soup spoon, gently hollow out the seeds and juice from the inside of the tomatoes. Reserve about ½ cup of the pulp, juice, and seeds (the "tomato liquid"). The majority of the tomato flesh should remain intact. Place hollow tomatoes in the baking dish.

When the rice is finished cooking and has cooled slightly, add garlic, basil, parsley, salt, and pepper to the cooked rice. Stir to combine. Spoon the seasoned rice equally into each tomato until all of the rice mix has been used. Pour about 1 tablespoon reserved tomato liquid and 1 teaspoon of olive oil onto the rice mix in each tomato. Place the tops back onto the tomatoes. Bake covered with foil or a lid for 60 minutes at 375°F. Let stand for about 5 minutes before serving.

# TWICE-BAKED SWEET POTATOES

These little boats of joy remind me of Thanksgiving every time I make them. They are a cross between a southern sweet potato casserole and my Aunt Gwen's sweet potato stacks.
Not only do they melt in your mouth, but they are also gluten-free and vegan! The toasted mini marshmallows and pecans make these sweet potatoes taste like dessert without blowing your diet.

**TOTAL TIME:** 75 minutes
**SERVINGS:** 16 twice-baked sweet potatoes
*TOTAL COST:* $6.06

## NUTRITIONAL INFORMATION

Calories: 105

Sodium: 28.7mg

Sugar: 9.9g

Total Fat: 3.2g

Carbohydrates: 18.9g

Protein: 1.7g

Saturated Fat: 1.1g

Fiber: 2.4g

Cholesterol: 3.9mg

## INGREDIENTS

9 5-inch sweet potatoes, scrubbed
¼ cup orange juice
¼ cup almond milk (if you don't have this, regular low-fat milk works well too)
2 tablespoons butter or vegan butter, such as Earth Balance
2 tablespoons brown sugar
1 teaspoon cinnamon
½ teaspoon nutmeg, freshly grated
A pinch of salt
100 mini marshmallows (about ½ of a standard bag)
⅓ cup pecans, chopped

## DIRECTIONS

Preheat oven to 400°F. Using a fork, poke a vent hole in each sweet potato. Lay potatoes on a rimmed baking sheet. Bake for 40–45 minutes or until the potatoes are soft when squeezed. Remove from the oven and let cool enough to handle. Keep the oven on.

Cut each sweet potato in half lengthwise. Scoop the flesh into a large mixing bowl, keeping the skin intact. Lay the skins out on the baking sheet for filling later. You will have 18 halves, but 2 will not be used (some fall apart). Eat or discard the extras. Add the orange juice, almond milk, butter, brown sugar, cinnamon, nutmeg, and a pinch of salt into the mixing bowl with the potato flesh. Combine with a mixer until smooth. Fill each skin with the sweet potato mixture.

Bake for 15 minutes and remove from the oven. Top each sweet potato with 1 teaspoon of pecans and 6–7 marshmallows. Turn on the broiler setting in the oven and broil sweet potatoes for 10–20 seconds or until golden brown. Turn on the light in your oven and watch the marshmallows toast, as they can burn easily. Remove from oven and serve hot.

## MAKE SWEET POTATO CASSEROLE INSTEAD!

**Follow the directions for combining the sweet potato filling. Transfer to a 13x9 baking dish and top with mini marshmallows and pecans. Bake for 15–20 minutes and serve.**

# YELLOW SQUASH CASSEROLE

I have to admit that I'm not usually the biggest fan of yellow squash, but I love them in this casserole! Substitute zucchini for the yellow squash, depending on what you have on hand.

**PREP TIME:** 30 minutes
**BAKE TIME:** 25 minutes
**SERVINGS:** 8, about 1 cup each
*TOTAL COST:* $8.05

## NUTRITIONAL INFORMATION

Calories: 146

Total Fat: 8.2g

Saturated Fat: 3.2g

Sodium: 258.8mg

Carbohydrates: 12.8g

Fiber: 3.1g

Sugar: 2.9g

Protein: 5.6g

Cholesterol: 7.5mg

## INGREDIENTS

4 medium or 2 large yellow squash

2 tablespoons olive oil, divided

2 medium red onions, sliced

Salt and pepper to season

2 tablespoons fresh sage, chopped

1 tablespoon fresh thyme, chopped

1 cup smoked Gouda or sharp cheddar cheese, shredded

15 whole wheat Ritz crackers, crumbled

## DIRECTIONS

To prepare your squash, cut the ends off of the squash, about a ½ inch from each end. Cut the squash in half lengthwise, scrape out the seeds and discard them. Slice the squash into ¼ inch half-moon-shaped slices and set aside. You should have about 8 cups of squash.

Preheat oven to 375°F and coat a 13x9 baking pan with cooking spray. In a large skillet, heat 1 tablespoon of olive oil over medium heat. Add the red onions and cook for about 7 minutes until soft. Place the onions in the prepared baking dish. Add the remaining 1 tablespoon of olive oil to the skillet and add the sliced squash. Season with salt and pepper. Cook for about 9 minutes or until soft. Add the chopped sage and thyme to the pan and cook for another minute. Remove from heat and add the squash mixture to the baking dish with the onions. Fold the mixture together so that the onions and squash are mixed and evenly distributed. Top with the shredded cheese and then the cracker crumbs. Bake for 25 minutes or until the crackers start to brown slightly.

# DESSERTS

# APPLE CRISP

My roommate, Erin, and I simply couldn't get enough apple crisp in our bellies during our college years. We would make a pan of it and eat the *entire pan* (no kidding there!). This was our favorite way to make a cheap and healthy dessert that also tasted amazing. Now, I wouldn't recommend eating the whole pan, but this recipe is so yummy that you will have trouble resisting a second scoop!

**PREP TIME:** 20 minutes
**BAKE TIME:** 40 minutes
**SERVINGS:** 10
**TOTAL COST:** $6.15

Pick up some low-fat vanilla frozen yogurt to turn this dessert into a sundae for under 300 calories.

## NUTRITIONAL INFORMATION

Calories: 188

Total Fat: 7g

Saturated Fat: 3.1g

Sodium: 5.3mg

Carbohydrates: 36.1g

Fiber: 3.2g

Sugar: 25.8g

Protein: 1.7g

Cholesterol: 12.4mg

## INGREDIENTS

10 small or 6 large Golden Delicious apples, peeled and cut into ¼-inch slices
½ cup all-purpose flour
¼ cup oats
½ cup brown sugar
1 teaspoon cinnamon
¼ cup (½ stick) unsalted butter, cold and cut into cubes
¼ cup walnuts

## DIRECTIONS

Preheat oven to 375°F. Spray a 13x9 baking dish or 10 small ramekins with cooking spray. Peel and slice apples and lay in the bottom of the prepared pan or ramekins. Set aside and prepare the topping.

In a large mixing bowl, combine the flour, oats, brown sugar, and cinnamon. Cut in the butter with a pastry blender or 2 knives until the butter chunks are no longer visible and the mixture resembles streusel. Stir in the walnuts. Spread the topping evenly over the apples and bake for 40 minutes in the center of the oven. Remove and let cool for 5 minutes before serving.

# BETTER-FOR-YOU BLUEBERRY POUND CAKE

For those dessert-lovers out there, some simple swaps will help you make your homemade baked goods healthier. Substituting half of the butter with yogurt and using finely ground whole wheat flour allowed me to make this pound cake *and* eat it too! People will be amazed that a giant satisfying piece of cake is only 255 calories without using artificial sweeteners. Feel free to use whatever berries you have on hand.

**PREP TIME:** 20 minutes   **BAKE TIME:** 75 or 50 minutes, depending on pan
**SERVINGS:** 16 slices
*TOTAL COST:* $6.79

### NUTRITIONAL INFORMATION

| | | |
|---|---|---|
| Calories: 257 | Sodium: 125.9mg | Sugar: 27.7g |
| Total Fat: 7.4g | Carbohydrates: 45g | Protein: 5.4g |
| Saturated Fat: 4.1g | Fiber: 3.2g | Cholesterol: 62mg |

### INGREDIENTS

½ cup unsalted butter, softened
½ cup low-fat vanilla Greek yogurt
2 cups sugar
4 eggs
1 teaspoon vanilla extract
3 cups finely ground white whole wheat flour (such as Wheat Montana), divided
½ teaspoon salt
1 teaspoon baking powder
1 pint fresh blueberries or 2 cups frozen blueberries

> If using frozen berries, stir them into the batter frozen. This prevents them from adding too much liquid to the batter prior to baking. They will thaw and bake in the oven.

> **Running low on vanilla Greek yogurt? Feel free to substitute it with plain Greek yogurt, regular vanilla yogurt, or a yogurt flavor that will complement the blueberry flavor well, like lemon or peach.**

## DIRECTIONS

Preheat oven to 325°F. Grease a large Bundt pan or 2 loaf pans generously with cooking spray. Cream the butter and Greek yogurt with an electric mixer. Add the sugar and beat until light and fluffy, about 3 minutes. Add the eggs one at a time, thoroughly mixing each egg in before adding the next. Beat in the vanilla extract.

In a separate bowl, combine 2 ½ cups whole wheat flour, salt, and baking powder. Gradually add it to the batter and beat until combined. Toss the blueberries with the remaining ½ cup whole wheat flour (this keeps the berries from sinking to the bottom of the batter as it bakes). Fold in the blueberries gently with a rubber spatula. Pour batter into the prepared pan and use a spatula to even out the batter in the pan. Bake for about 75 minutes for a Bundt pan or 50 minutes if using 2 loaf pans. It is done when an inserted toothpick comes out clean. Let the cake rest in the pan for about 5 minutes.

Use a butter knife to gently release the sides of the cake from the pan. Place a plate or serving tray on top of the pan and flip to fully release the cake. It may not come out immediately, so let it sit until it comes out on its own. Slice and serve with coffee or tea.

If you can't find white whole wheat flour or finely ground whole wheat flour, you can substitute this amount with 1 ½ cups all-purpose flour and 1 ½ cups stone ground whole wheat flour.

# AUNT CAROL'S FRESH APPLE CAKE

My Aunt Carol Jahnke makes the most delicious spice cake with fresh apples studded throughout. To make-over her recipe, I replaced half of the oil with applesauce, which actually costs exactly the same price. I also reduced the amount of sugar by ½ cup but increased the amount of vanilla extract by 1 teaspoon, which is another healthy baking tip to reduce calories yet maintain flavor.

**PREP TIME:** 20 minutes    **BAKE TIME:** 35–40 minutes

**SERVINGS:** 12 slices

**TOTAL COST:** $5.90

## NUTRITIONAL INFORMATION

| | | |
|---|---|---|
| Calories: 258 | Sodium: 222.3mg | Sugar: 32g |
| Total Fat: 5.8g | Carbohydrates: 49.7g | Protein: 3.3g |
| Saturated Fat: 3.6g | Fiber: 1.8g | Cholesterol: 31mg |

## INGREDIENTS

Shortening and flour for greasing

1 ½ cups sugar

¼ cup vegetable or canola oil

¼ cup unsweetened applesauce

2 eggs

2 teaspoons vanilla

4 cups apples (about 4 large apples), peeled and diced, divided

2 cups all-purpose flour

2 teaspoons cinnamon

2 teaspoons baking soda

3 tablespoons powdered sugar

## DIRECTIONS

Preheat oven to 400°F. Grease a 13x9 cake pan with shortening and then dust with flour. Set aside.

In the base of a stand mixer or a large mixing bowl, combine the sugar, oil, applesauce, eggs, vanilla, and 1 cup of apples. Beat until all of the ingredients are well combined. Scrape down the sides of the bowl once and continue to mix on low while you prepare the remaining ingredients.

In a separate small bowl, stir together the flour, cinnamon, and baking soda. Add to the wet ingredients in the mixer. Add in the remaining 3 cups of apple with the mixer on the lowest speed, or fold in by hand. Pour the batter into the prepared pan and bake for 35–40 minutes. The finished cake will be brown on the top and will begin the pull away from the sides of the pan. Let cool completely. Dust with powdered sugar before serving.

# VANILLA COCONUT CREAM CAKE

I love make-ahead easy desserts, and this is surely one of them! You can actually use whatever type of cake mix, soda, and pudding mix you prefer.

**PREP TIME:** 15 minutes   **BAKE TIME:** 18–20 minutes   **COOL TIME:** 30 minutes
**SERVINGS:** 15 slices
**TOTAL COST:** $6.64

## NUTRITIONAL INFORMATION

Calories: 235
Total Fat: 5.9g
Saturated Fat: 3.4g

Sodium: 366.1mg
Carbohydrates: 43.6g
Fiber: 0.7g

Sugar: 11.9g
Protein: 3.5g
Cholesterol: 2.4mg

## INGREDIENTS

18-ounce yellow cake mix
12-ounce can cream soda or Coke
3.4-ounce package instant vanilla pudding
   mix
1-ounce package fat-free instant vanilla
   pudding mix

3 cups cold low-fat milk
8-ounce tub of light whipped topping
1 teaspoon coconut extract
½ cup shredded sweetened flaked coconut

## DIRECTIONS

Preheat oven to 350°F. Grease a 13x9 cake pan with cooking spray on the bottom and sides. In a large bowl, whisk together the cake mix and cream soda until all of the visible cake mix is mixed in. You will still see some small lumps in the batter. Pour into the prepared pan and spread evenly. Bake for 18–20 minutes or until a toothpick comes out clean. Let the cake cool completely, about 30 minutes.

In a medium bowl, whisk together the pudding mixes and milk for about 2 minutes. Let the pudding set for about 5 minutes. Empty the whipped topping into another medium bowl and fold in the coconut extract and shredded coconut. Set aside.

Once the cake has fully cooled, use a butter knife to poke holes throughout the cake. Spread on the pudding and gently push some of the pudding into the holes with your spatula. Top the cake with the coconut whipped cream. Refrigerate until ready to serve.

# LAUREN K'S SOFT CHOCOLATE CHIP COOKIES

This is my #1 most-requested recipe of all time. Everyone falls in love with these cookies upon the first bite. I teach this recipe to every class of students I instruct, and I challenge them to find a rival recipe. No one has succeeded yet! This recipe features white whole wheat flour and, with its mix-in variations, it will please any taste or desire. Use my ideas or create your own!

**PREP TIME:** 20 minutes plus 1 hour chill time    **BAKE TIME:** 8–9 minutes per batch

**SERVINGS:** 50 cookies

**TOTAL COST:** $6.03

## NUTRITIONAL INFORMATION

| | | |
|---|---|---|
| Calories: 120 | Sodium: 59.7mg | Sugar: 12.4g |
| Total Fat: 6.6g | Carbohydrates: 17g | Protein: 1.8g |
| Saturated Fat: 3.8g | Fiber: 0.6g | Cholesterol: 16.7mg |

## INGREDIENTS

1 cup (2 sticks) unsalted butter, softened (no substitutions)
¾ cup brown sugar
¾ cup granulated sugar
1 egg
2 teaspoons vanilla

2 ½ cups finely ground white whole wheat flour, such as Wheat Montana
1 teaspoon baking soda
½ teaspoon salt
11.5-ounce bag of milk chocolate chips or see the variations to the right to mix it up

## DIRECTIONS

If you want these cookies to be perfect, you must follow the directions word for word!

In a large mixing bowl, cream the butter, brown sugar, and granulated sugar together with an electric mixer until light and fluffy. Add the egg and vanilla and beat to combine for about 1 minute. This mixture will look like light brown cake icing.

In a separate medium bowl, combine the whole wheat flour, baking soda, and salt. Stir to combine. Add the flour mixture to the butter mixture all at once. STIR BY HAND WITH A WOODEN SPOON UNTIL THE FLOUR MIXTURE IS FULLY COMBINED. It will be stiff dough. Do not be tempted to save time by using the electric mixer to mix in the flour. Hand stirring will make the cookies more soft and chewy. Stir in the milk chocolate chips (or your favorite mix-in) by hand. Chill dough in the refrigerator for at least 1 hour and up to 48 hours in advance.

To bake the cookies, preheat oven to 350°F and line 2 baking sheets with parchment paper. Cut the paper to fit the size of the pan to prevent the parchment from burning. Drop 1-inch balls of dough onto the baking sheet and stagger to promote even baking. Don't mold the dough too much with your hands; the heat from your hands will melt the butter and make your cookies hard. Bake for 8–9 minutes or until you see golden-brown tips on the cookies. Remove from the oven and let them sit on the baking sheet for a minute to fully set and then remove to a cooling rack. Store cookies in an airtight container to keep them soft!

## VARIATIONS
**You can replace the milk chocolate chips with any 2 cups of mix-ins you'd like.**

- 2 cups plain M&Ms
- 1 cup peanut butter chips + 1 cup chopped Reese's Peanut Butter Cups
- 1 cup white chocolate chips + 1 cup dried cranberries
- 1 cup mint chips + 1 cup dark chocolate chips
- 1 cup butterscotch chips + 1 cup toffee bits
- 1 cup semisweet chocolate chips + 1 cup chopped pecans

# WHITE CHOCOLATE COCONUT BISCOTTI

Because of my Italian family roots, biscotti and hot tea are hallmarks from my childhood. Biscotti are baked twice for a perfect texture for dipping into a hot beverage. My grandmother, Helen Bucci, made the best anise-flavored biscotti I've ever tasted; her creations inspired me to experiment with my own variations. This is a modern favorite of mine, with flecks of coconut and chunks of white chocolate. With the whole wheat flour and spices I've added, you'll enjoy eating a dessert that you can feel good about. No guilt here!

**PREP TIME:** 15 minutes    **BAKE TIME:** 30 minutes plus 10 minutes
**SERVINGS:** 30 biscotti
**TOTAL COST:** $3.81

## NUTRITIONAL INFORMATION

Calories: 115            Sodium: 69.3mg           Sugar: 7.5g
Total Fat: 3.5g          Carbohydrates: 18.1g     Protein: 2.8g
Saturated Fat: 2.1g      Fiber: 1.2g              Cholesterol: 25.4mg

## INGREDIENTS

2 cups all-purpose flour
1 cup finely ground white whole wheat flour, such as Wheat Montana
2 teaspoons baking powder
¼ teaspoon salt
1 cup sugar
1 teaspoon vanilla extract
4 eggs
2 tablespoons vegetable or canola oil
½ cup sweetened flaked coconut
½ cup white chocolate chips

## DIRECTIONS

Preheat your oven to 350°F. Line 2 baking sheets with parchment paper and set aside. In a small mixing bowl, combine the all-purpose flour, whole wheat flour, baking powder, and salt. Stir and set aside.

In a large mixing bowl, mix together the sugar, vanilla, eggs, and vegetable oil with an electric mixer. Add in the flour mixture and mix until a stiff, sticky dough forms. The dough will be very thick. Mix in the coconut and white chocolate chips. Separate the dough into 2 balls. Form each dough ball into a long log, about 12 inches by 4 inches, on the parchment paper on the prepared baking sheet. Bake for 30 minutes. Remove from the oven and let cool.

Once the logs are room temperature, increase the oven temperature to 400°F. Use a serrated knife to slice the logs on the bias, about ½-inch thick each. You should get about 15 slices from each log. Lay the slices out on the baking sheet and bake for 5 minutes. Flip over the biscotti and bake on the opposite side for 5 additional minutes. Remove from the oven and let cool. Enjoy with a hot cup of tea or coffee. Keep in a sealed container for up to 2 weeks.

## FOR A SOFTER COOKIE:

Bake for 5 minutes at 400°F and remove from the oven. Do not bake for an additional 5 minutes.

## FOR A HARDER COOKIE:

Bake for 7 minutes on each side.

# RUSTIC STONE-FRUIT TART

My Uncle Gale and Aunt Dawn Roland have a peach orchard that produces some of the best peaches I've ever tasted. I love to use those peaches, along with other summer fruits like plums and apricots, and turn them into scrumptious desserts like this one. Using only half of a store-bought pie crust to make a rustic tart not only simplifies the process of assembling a whole fruit pie, but also saves money.

**PREP TIME:** 15 minutes    **BAKE TIME:** 28–30 minutes
**SERVINGS:** 8 slices
*TOTAL COST:* $5.75

## NUTRITIONAL INFORMATION

Calories: 181

Sodium: 143mg

Sugar: 16.2g

Total Fat: 7.2g

Carbohydrates: 32.2g

Protein: 1.8g

Saturated Fat: 3g

Fiber: 1.5g

Cholesterol: 5mg

## INGREDIENTS

3 ½ cups fresh stone fruit, like peaches, plums, or apricots, sliced

¼ cup brown sugar

1 teaspoon cinnamon

Juice of ½ lemon

3 tablespoons flour, plus more for dusting the counter

1 store-bought unbaked pie crust (they usually come in boxes of 2, but you will only use one for this dessert)

1 tablespoon milk

## DIRECTIONS

Preheat oven to 375°F. Line a rimmed baking sheet with parchment paper. In a large mixing bowl, add the sliced stone fruit, brown sugar, cinnamon, lemon juice, and flour. Gently fold the mixture together to combine and coat the fruit slices.

Take the pie crust out of the plastic and gently unroll it onto a lightly floured surface. Use a rolling pin to roll the crust out flat about ½ inch larger than the original size. Roll the crust onto the rolling pin for easy transfer and place the crust onto the parchment paper. Gently lay the fruit filling in the middle of the crust and spread it out, leaving a 1-inch border of crust. Use your fingers to fold the 1-inch border of crust over the filling, pressing any open holes or cracks together. Brush the crust with milk—this makes it golden and shiny after baking.

Bake the tart for 28–30 minutes or until the filling is set and the crust is golden brown. Remove from the oven and let cool for 10 minutes. Cut into 8 slices and serve.

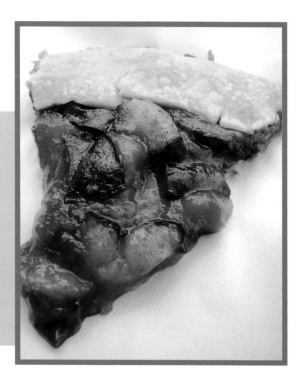

## RUSTIC TART VARIATIONS

**APPLE:** Use 3 ½ cups peeled and sliced apples and decrease the flour to 2 tablespoons.

**BLUEBERRY:** Use 3 ½ cups fresh blueberries and increase the flour to ¼ cup.

# S'MORES PIE

If I had to pick a favorite dessert flavor profile, s'mores would be the hands down winner for me. I'll eat campfire s'mores, s'mores ice cream, s'mores cookies, and *s'mores pie*. This is one of the easiest, fastest, and s'more-licious desserts you will ever make!

**TOTAL TIME:** 10 minutes
**SERVINGS:** 8 slices
*TOTAL COST:* $5.76

## NUTRITIONAL INFORMATION

Calories: 246
Total Fat: 9.3g
Saturated Fat: 3.8g

Sodium: 283.9mg
Carbohydrates: 35.8g
Fiber: 0.4g

Sugar: 24.8g
Protein: 4g
Cholesterol: 3.7mg

## INGREDIENTS

5.9-ounce package of instant chocolate pudding mix
2 ½ cups low-fat milk
2 cups or 8-ounce container light whipped topping
1 premade 9-inch graham cracker crust
2 cups mini marshmallows

## DIRECTIONS

Arrange a rack in your oven so that it is about 6 inches away from the top and then turn on the oven broiler. In a medium mixing bowl, whisk together the chocolate pudding mix and the milk until smooth. Set aside for 2 minutes or until set. Fold in the whipped topping with a rubber spatula and pour into the graham cracker crust. Top with mini marshmallows. Broil for 30 seconds or until marshmallows are toasted. Keep an eye on the pie, as the marshmallows can burn quickly. Remove from the oven and refrigerate until ready to serve.

# NO-BAKE PUMPKIN CHEESECAKE

Nothing screams "Thanksgiving" like this dessert! No need to slave over a homemade crust or to consume loads of calories and fat. This slice of heaven will cause everyone at your table to give thanks to *you* . . . for ending their holiday meal with a guilt-free sweet treat!

**PREP TIME:** 15 minutes     **CHILL TIME:** 4 hours
**SERVINGS:** 8 slices
*TOTAL COST:* $6.97

## NUTRITIONAL INFORMATION

Calories: 280                 Sodium: 426.8mg              Sugar: 18.3g
Total Fat: 12.7g              Carbohydrates: 36.3g         Protein: 6.2g
Saturated Fat: 6.4g          Fiber: 2.3g                  Cholesterol: 23.4mg

## INGREDIENTS

8 ounces light cream cheese, room temperature
1 cup pumpkin puree
1 teaspoon pumpkin pie spice, plus more for sprinkling on top
1 4-serving package of instant vanilla or cheesecake pudding mix
1 ½ cups low-fat milk
2 cups light whipped topping, divided
1 premade 9-inch graham cracker crust

## DIRECTIONS

In a large mixing bowl, combine the light cream cheese, pumpkin, and pumpkin pie spice with an electric mixer until smooth. Add the pudding mix and milk and mix again with the mixer until the mixture is thoroughly combined and no lumps of cream cheese are visible. Fold in 1 cup of the whipped topping with a rubber spatula. Pour into the graham cracker crust. Spread 1 additional cup of whipped topping evenly over the top of the pumpkin mix. Cover and refrigerate for 4 hours or overnight. Before serving, sprinkle additional pumpkin pie spice over the top of the pie for garnish.

*also if using dairy-free milk*

# BANANA ICE CREAM

This recipe features *two* ingredients to make an all-natural "ice cream" with no sugar or cream to be found. My husband requests it at least two nights a week, although he would have it every night if I made it. Check out my mix-in ideas for some different flavors!

**FREEZE TIME (IN ADVANCE):** 2–3 hours
**ACTIVE TIME:** 10 minutes
**SERVINGS:** 4, ⅔ cup each
**TOTAL COST:** $1.23

## NUTRITIONAL INFORMATION

Calories: 134

Total Fat: 0.8g

Saturated Fat: 0.4g

Sodium: 15.2mg

Carbohydrates: 32.6g

Fiber: 3.5g

Sugar: 18.3g

Protein: 2.5g

Cholesterol: 1.5mg

## INGREDIENTS

4 ripe bananas

½ cup low-fat milk or a dairy-free milk of your choice

## DIRECTIONS

Peel and cut the bananas into ¼ inch slices. Lay them out evenly on a baking sheet. Freeze for 2–3 hours or until banana slices are completely frozen.

Scrape banana slices off the baking sheet with a sturdy spatula into a food processor. Pulse about 10 times. Add half of the milk and pulse 10 more times. Stream in the remaining milk and run the processor for about 10 more seconds or until the mixture looks like ice cream. Stir or pulse in your mix-ins, if using. Enjoy immediately or freeze until ready to eat.

# MIX-IT-IN
## FOR UNDER 70 CALORIES PER SERVING

**COCONUT WHITE CHOCOLATE:** 2 tablespoons shredded sweetened coconut + 2 tablespoons white chocolate chips

**OREO:** 4 Oreo cookies

**CHOCOLATE PEANUT BUTTER:** 2 tablespoons milk chocolate chips + 1 tablespoon natural peanut butter

**CHOCOLATE COVERED CHERRY:** ½ cup frozen pitted cherries + 2 tablespoons dark chocolate chips

**S'MORES:** 1 graham cracker sheet broken into pieces, 2 tablespoons milk chocolate chips, and ½ cup mini marshmallows (stir in with spoon)

**PROTEIN ICE CREAM:** 2 scoops of your favorite protein powder (sprinkled over the frozen sliced bananas in the food processor before pulsing)

# DIY
## SNACKS, BEVERAGES, SPREADS, DRESSINGS & OTHER RECIPES

HAPPY FACE RICE CAKES

CREAMY PUMPKIN DIP
*WITH FUN DIPPERS*

EASY FRUIT KABOBS

LAUGHING COW PRETZELS

SPICED PECANS

SIMPLE STOVETOP
POPCORN
*WITH HOMEMADE
SEASONING MIXES*

BLACKBERRY LEMONADE

ALMOND JOY CREAMER

30-CALORIE CHAI
TEA LATTE

PUMPKIN BUTTER

APRICOT PEACH COMPOTE

POOR MAN'S PESTO

LBJ BARBECUE SAUCE

SWEET GARLIC BBQ SAUCE

ROASTED GARLIC

DILLED RANCH DRESSING

GRAM BUCCI'S ITALIAN
VINAIGRETTE

CREAMY POPPY SEED
DRESSING

CAESAR DRESSING

HONEY MUSTARD
DRESSING

THOUSAND ISLAND
DRESSING

ASIAN VINAIGRETTE

# HAPPY FACE RICE CAKES

My husband, Bryan, and his cousin Brett love to eat protein-packed rice cakes before they exercise. It gives them a quick energy boost to get them through their cardio and weight training sessions and some protein to help rebuild muscle. You can add whatever toppings you'd like, but we like natural nut butters the best!

**TOTAL TIME:** 5 minutes
**SERVINGS:** 2 rice cake faces
*TOTAL COST:* $0.82

## NUTRITIONAL INFORMATION

Calories: 187
Total Fat: 10.1g
Saturated Fat: 2.1g

Sodium: 81.3mg
Carbohydrates: 22g
Fiber: 1g

Sugar: 10.2g
Protein: 4.9g
Cholesterol: 1.3mg

## INGREDIENTS

2 large chocolate, apple, or caramel flavored rice cakes
2 tablespoons natural peanut butter or almond butter
6 chocolate chips
20 mini marshmallows

## DIRECTIONS

Spread 1 tablespoon of natural peanut butter or almond butter onto each rice cake. Use the chocolate chips to make 2 eyes and a nose. Use 10 marshmallows to make the mouth on each rice cake. Eat your snack with a friend!

# CREAMY PUMPKIN DIP
## WITH FUN DIPPERS

I always enjoy healthy dips with apples as an afternoon snack or a late-night treat. Although this is especially perfect for the holiday season, it tastes great all year long!

**TOTAL TIME:** 7 minutes
**SERVINGS:** 12, 2 tablespoons each
*TOTAL COST:* $2.24

### NUTRITIONAL INFORMATION

Calories: 46

Total Fat: 1.7g

Saturated Fat: 1g

Sodium: 51.9mg

Carbohydrates: 6.8g

Fiber: 0.4g

Sugar: 6.2g

Protein: 1.7g

Cholesterol: 6.7mg

### INGREDIENTS

½ cup pumpkin puree

½ cup low-fat vanilla Greek yogurt

4 ounces light cream cheese, room temperature

1 teaspoon pumpkin pie spice

3 tablespoons brown sugar

### DIRECTIONS

In a medium-sized bowl, blend all ingredients with an electric mixer until smooth. Serve with your favorite dippers.

### 70-CALORIE DIPPERS:

- 1 small apple, sliced
- 5 vanilla wafers
- 1 sheet of graham crackers broken into 4 crackers
- 12 teddy grahams

# EASY FRUIT KABOBS

Fruit kabobs are always a big hit with kids and adults alike. These are some of my favorite fruits that are affordable all year long, but feel free to substitute your own favorites, like pineapple, cantaloupe, plums, blueberries, or nectarines.

**TOTAL TIME:** 10 minutes
**SERVINGS:** 18 kabobs, 1 kabob per serving
*TOTAL COST:* $4.82

## NUTRITIONAL INFORMATION

Calories: 27

Total Fat: 0.1g

Saturated Fat: 0g

Sodium: 0.6mg

Carbohydrates: 7.0g

Fiber:   1.1g

Sugar: 5.7g

Protein: 0.3g

Cholesterol: 0mg

## INGREDIENTS

2 large navel oranges, peeled
2 cups dark purple seedless grapes
2 large Granny Smith or Golden Delicious apples
18 wooden kabob skewers

## No kabob skewers on hand?

Make a fruit salad instead!

## DIRECTIONS

Cut the orange segments and apples into 1-inch pieces. There should be 25 equal pieces of each type of fruit. Skewer on the oranges, grapes and apples alternately until all of the fruit is used. Serve or refrigerate.

# LAUGHING COW PRETZELS

**TOTAL TIME:** 5 minutes
**SERVINGS:** 1
*TOTAL COST:* $0.63

## NUTRITIONAL INFORMATION

| | | |
|---|---|---|
| Calories: 155 | Sodium: 600mg | Sugar: 2g |
| Total Fat: 2.5g | Carbohydrates: 26g | Protein: 5g |
| Saturated Fat: 1g | Fiber: 1g | Cholesterol: 4.5mg |

## INGREDIENTS

1 serving of pretzel snaps, about 24 pretzels

1 wedge of Laughing Cow cheese, like French Onion or Garlic & Herb

## DIRECTIONS

Use the pretzels to scoop up the cheese. It's that easy!

# SPICED PECANS

I enjoy snacking on spiced nuts from festivals, but they are pricey and covered in sugar. My friend, Susan Sachs, came up with a recipe that is much more health conscious and just as delicious. We also bag them up to give as gifts around Christmas time—making for an affordable and tasty gift from the heart.

**PREP TIME:** 8 minutes
**BAKE TIME:** 60 minutes
**SERVINGS:** 16, ¼ cup each
*TOTAL COST:* $7.89

## NUTRITIONAL INFORMATION

| | | |
|---|---|---|
| Calories: 205 | Sodium: 76.4mg | Sugar: 4.9g |
| Total Fat: 19.5g | Carbohydrates: 8.3g | Protein: 2.7g |
| Saturated Fat: 1.7g | Fiber: 3.1g | Cholesterol: 0mg |

## INGREDIENTS

4 cups pecan halves
⅓ cup sugar
2 tablespoons cinnamon
½ teaspoon salt
½ teaspoon nutmeg

½ teaspoon pumpkin pie spice
¼ teaspoon allspice or cloves
1 egg white
1 tablespoon water

## DIRECTIONS

Preheat oven to 250°F and coat a large rimmed baking sheet with cooking spray. Lay the pecans out on the sheet in an even layer.

In a small mixing bowl, combine the sugar, cinnamon, salt, nutmeg, pumpkin pie spice, and allspice. Add the egg white and water and whisk together until a thick liquid develops. Pour the mixture over the pecans and toss with your hands to coat the nuts completely.

Bake the pecans in the oven for 1 hour, tossing with a spatula every 15 minutes. Let cool and store in an air tight container.

## OPTIONS AND IDEAS

**SALAD TOPPERS:** Break the spiced pecans into pieces and top your favorite salad, like my Strawberry Spinach Salad on p. 96.

**TRAIL MIX:** Combine the spiced pecans with dried cranberries, pumpkin seeds, and dried apricots.

**BAKED SWEET POTATO TOPPER:** Top a baked sweet potato with spiced pecan pieces, a little butter, and a sprinkle of brown sugar.

# SIMPLE STOVE TOP POPCORN
## WITH HOMEMADE SEASONING MIXES

Popcorn is one of my favorite snacks! I love it so much that I sometimes eat it for lunch, too. Although I keep bags of popcorn on hand, nothing tastes quite like homemade popcorn. The recipe below is for use on the stove. You can use a popcorn machine or a microwave popping bowl with the Seasoning Mix Options too. Pop some right now, sit back, and enjoy your favorite movie.

**TOTAL TIME:** 5–7 minutes
**SERVINGS:** 2, about 3.5 cups each
**TOTAL COST:** $0.35 (Traditional) or about $1.00 (with seasoning mix)

**NUTRITIONAL INFORMATION** (Traditional)
*All of the seasoning mixes options will add less than 55 calories per serving to the Traditional Recipe.*

| | | |
|---|---|---|
| Calories: 147 | Sodium: 1.1mg | Sugar: 0g |
| Total Fat: 5.7g | Carbohydrates: 21.8g | Protein: 3.4g |
| Saturated Fat: 0.8g | Fiber: 4.2g | Cholesterol: 0mg |

**INGREDIENTS** (Traditional)
¼ cup popcorn kernels                    Salt and pepper to season
2 teaspoons olive oil

**DIRECTIONS**

Pour the popcorn kernels into a 2-quart saucepan with a tight-fitting lid. Pour the olive oil over the kernels and season with salt and pepper. If using one of the seasoning mixes to the right, sprinkle the seasoning mix onto the unpopped kernels inside the pot. Shake a few times to cover the kernels in the oil and seasonings. Put the lid on the popcorn and turn the heat on medium. Shake about every 10 seconds until you hear the kernels begin to pop. Once popping begins, shake frequently to keep the kernels moving and prevent the popped popcorn from burning. Continue to shake over the heat until you can count 2 full seconds between pops. Remove from heat and pour into serving bowls. Sprinkle the popcorn with additional salt or ingredients from the Seasoning Mix Options, and serve hot.

## SEASONING MIX OPTIONS

**Combine the ingredients in a small bowl for seasoning your popcorn. You can multiply the recipes below and store leftovers in an empty spice container for another day.**

**CAJUN CURRY SEASONING:** 1 teaspoon Old Bay seasoning and ¼ teaspoon curry powder

**SUGAR AND SPICE:** 2 teaspoons brown sugar, ¼ teaspoon cinnamon, ¼ teaspoon nutmeg, and ¼ teaspoon paprika

**SMOKY SEASONING:** ¼ teaspoon garlic powder, ¼ teaspoon onion powder, and ½ teaspoon Montreal Steak Seasoning

**ITALIAN BLEND:** ¼ teaspoon dried oregano, ¼ teaspoon dried basil, ¼ teaspoon dried parsley, and ¼ teaspoon garlic powder, plus 1 tablespoon of grated parmesan cheese on top of hot popped popcorn

**KETTLE CORN:** 1 tablespoon white sugar and ¼ teaspoon salt

# BLACKBERRY LEMONADE

Few things are better than an ice-cold glass of lemonade on a hot day. A few years ago, I went berry picking and had a ridiculous amount of blackberries that I couldn't use up fast enough . . . so, Blackberry Lemonade was born! Feel free to sweeten the lemonade with sugar, maple syrup, or a sweetener of your choice instead of honey.

**TOTAL TIME:** 10 minutes
**SERVINGS:** 7, 8 ounces each
*TOTAL COST:* $3.50

### NUTRITIONAL INFORMATION

| | | |
|---|---|---|
| Calories: 85 | Sodium: 1.2mg | Sugar: 21.1g |
| Total Fat: 0g | Carbohydrates: 23.4g | Protein: 0.2g |
| Saturated Fat: 0g | Fiber: 0.7g | Cholesterol: 0mg |

### INGREDIENTS

6 cups water, divided
½ cup honey
4 lemons, juice completely squeezed and strained

1 cup fresh blackberries
Ice for serving

### DIRECTIONS

In a small saucepan, make a simple syrup with 2 cups of water and the honey. Simmer the mixture over low heat to dissolve the honey, stirring frequently. As the syrup heats, juice your lemons. Squeeze out all of the juice into a small bowl, using a juicer or a reamer to get out the most juice. Place a fine mesh strainer over a serving pitcher and pour the juice into the pitcher through the strainer to remove all seeds and pulp.

Place the berries in the small bowl and muddle them to extract the juice. Use a potato masher or your hands for this. Place the mixture in the strainer on the pitcher and press as much juice through as you can. Discard pulp (or eat it! It is a perfect mix-in for oatmeal or yogurt.). Add in the simple syrup and 4 additional cups of cold water. Stir well to combine. Load glasses with ice, pour in the lemonade, and enjoy! Keep refrigerated if not serving immediately.

## CLOTHING TIP:

**Wear an apron when making this lemonade . . . the first time I made this, my shirt was speckled with blackberry juice after swishing the berries.**

# ALMOND JOY CREAMER

I love to try different bottled creamers to flavor my hot beverages, but, when I look at the label, the additives and preservatives that I can't pronounce scare me. This creamer reminds me of an Almond Joy candy bar without all of the mystery ingredients, plus, it costs about the same as the store-bought version!

**TOTAL TIME:** 5 minutes
**MAKES:** 2 cups   **SERVINGS:** 32, 1 tablespoon each
*TOTAL COST:* $2.05

## NUTRITIONAL INFORMATION

Calories: 24
Total Fat: 1.5g
Saturated Fat: 1g

Sodium: 4.5mg
Carbohydrates: 2.3g
Fiber: 0g

Sugar: 2.1g
Protein: 0.4g
Cholesterol: 5.3mg

## INGREDIENTS
1 ¾ cups half and half
¼ cup pure maple syrup
1 tablespoon Hershey's cocoa powder
1 teaspoon almond extract
1 teaspoon coconut extract

## DIRECTIONS

In a small saucepan over low heat, combine all 5 ingredients and whisk vigorously for about 1 minute until the cocoa powder dissolves. Heat through until the mixture steams. Do not boil. Use a funnel to pour the mixture into a glass storage jar and keep refrigerated for up to 2 weeks. Stir into your favorite coffee or hot tea beverage. Gently shake the sealed creamer container before each use.

# 30-CALORIE CHAI TEA LATTE

This is how Lauren K starts her day! It's so simple and delicious. With this new trick on hand, you can leave those 300-calorie, 4-dollar lattes at the drive thru and make your own in about 5 minutes.

**TOTAL TIME:** 5 minutes
**SERVINGS:** 1, 16 ounces
*TOTAL COST:* $0.41

## NUTRITIONAL INFORMATION

Calories: 30

Total Fat: 1.5g

Saturated Fat: 1g

Sodium: 4.5mg

Carbohydrates: 2.3g

Fiber: 0g

Sugar: 2.1g

Protein: 0.4g

Cholesterol: 5.3mg

## INGREDIENTS

1 ½ cups boiling water

½ cup original almond milk

1 chai spice tea bag

½ or 1 full packet of stevia, depending on desired sweetness

## DIRECTIONS

Bring water to a boil. Meanwhile, heat the almond milk for 1 minute on high in the microwave in a microwave-safe travel mug or extra-large coffee cup. Once the water boils, pour the water into the mug to fill it up. Add the tea bag and steep for 2–3 minutes. Remove tea bag and add in stevia. Stir and enjoy!

# PUMPKIN BUTTER

I fell in love with pumpkin butter when I tasted it at an Amish store in Danville, Pennsylvania. I've since found and adapted a recipe from skinnytaste.com that I make over the holidays, both for my own use and to jar as gifts for others.

**TOTAL TIME:** 45 minutes
**MAKES:** about 3 ⅓ cups    **SERVINGS:** 50, about 1 tablespoon each
**TOTAL COST:** $5.31

### NUTRITIONAL INFORMATION

Calories: 15          Sodium: 1.6mg          Sugar: 3.2g
Total Fat: 0.1g       Carbohydrates: 4.3g    Protein: 0.3g
Saturated Fat: 0g     Fiber: 0.7g            Cholesterol: 0mg

### INGREDIENTS

28 ounces pumpkin puree          ¾ cup apple juice or apple cider
1 teaspoon vanilla extract       2 teaspoons pumpkin pie spice
½ cup brown sugar                3 cinnamon sticks

### DIRECTIONS

Combine all of the ingredients above in a medium saucepan and simmer over low heat for 30 minutes or until thick, like apple butter. Stir every 5 minutes. Ladle into mason jars and seal tightly. Refrigerate for up to 2 weeks.

## USING YOUR PUMPKIN BUTTER

- Use as a dip for apples or grapes
- Spread on a piece of whole grain bread or an English muffin
- Stir into hot oatmeal
- Dollop onto frozen yogurt
- Stir into Greek yogurt and top with granola

# APRICOT PEACH COMPOTE

One of my high school teachers, Linda Shrader, recently treated my sister and me to Sunday brunch at Crazy Alice's Café in Somerset, Pennsylvania. They served homemade ginger peach apricot compote as a topper for their wheat berry French toast. It was hot, sweet, and oh-so-delicious! I couldn't wait to get home and recreate that wonderful fruit delight. Spoon it over pancakes, French toast, or waffles, or use it as a topper for Greek yogurt, hot oatmeal, or ice cream.

**TOTAL TIME:** 20 minutes
**SERVINGS:** 10, ¼ cup each
**TOTAL COST:** $5.34

## NUTRITIONAL INFORMATION

Calories: 62
Total Fat: 0.2g
Saturated Fat: 0.2g

Sodium: 6.3mg
Carbohydrates: 16.2g
Fiber: 1.1g

Sugar: 14.5g
Protein: 0.5g
Cholesterol: 0mg

## INGREDIENTS

2 cups peaches, peeled and cubed (about 3 large peaches)
1 cup apricots, cubed (about 4 large apricots)
⅓ cup orange marmalade
⅓ cup water
2 tablespoons honey
1 teaspoon pumpkin pie spice

## DIRECTIONS

Combine all ingredients in a medium saucepan. Bring to a boil and then turn the heat down and simmer for 10 minutes, stirring occasionally. Serve hot, or cool completely and store in an airtight container for up to 1 week. To use, simply reheat the portion you desire.

# POOR MAN'S PESTO

I am a pesto-aholic. I smear pesto on just about anything, including pizza, omelets, sandwiches, and potato salad. Traditional pesto features basil and pine nuts, which can rack up the grocery bill. My version not only saves money by replacing expensive pine nuts with walnuts, but also packs handfuls of healthy spinach into the spread as well. I like to make this recipe, use it for one dish, and store it in the refrigerator for later use in other recipes, like Pesto Prosciutto Pizza (p. 134) or Italian Paisan Burgers (p. 152).

**TOTAL TIME:** 5 minutes
**MAKES:** 2 cups   **SERVINGS:** 32, 1 tablespoon each
**TOTAL COST:** $6.64

## NUTRITIONAL INFORMATION

Calories: 30
Total Fat: 2.8g
Saturated Fat: 0.6g

Sodium: 4.96mg
Carbohydrates: 0.4g
Fiber: 0.2g

Sugar: 0.1g
Protein: 0.9g
Cholesterol: 1.2mg

## INGREDIENTS

3 cups loosely packed spinach or 10 ounces frozen chopped spinach, thoroughly drained
1 cup loosely packed fresh basil or ¾-ounce package fresh basil
1 garlic clove, roughly chopped
Juice of ½ lemon
½ cup parmesan cheese
½ cup walnuts
¼ teaspoon salt
¼ cup olive oil

### MAKE SOME PISTACHIO PEA-STO INSTEAD!

Replace the spinach with 16 ounces thawed green peas and substitute the walnuts with shelled pistachios.

## DIRECTIONS

Plug in a large food processor and line up the blade inside the bowl before adding ingredients. You can make your pesto in a blender if you don't have a food processor.

Add spinach, basil, garlic, lemon juice, parmesan cheese, walnuts, and salt into the food processor. Pulse 5 times and run the food processor until the mixture is mostly pureed. Stream in the olive oil and set the food processor to run for about 30 seconds until the ingredients are thoroughly incorporated. Scrape ingredients stuck to the side of the bowl back down into the mix if needed and run for 5 additional seconds. Taste and season with additional salt if desired. Use in your favorite recipe or store in an airtight container in the refrigerator for up to 2 weeks.

# LBJ BARBECUE SAUCE

Barbecue chicken was a family favorite at my Pap Pap's house on Sunday afternoons. I believe there were two ingredients that made his chicken better than any other: love and his homemade barbecue sauce. Named after my grandfather's visit to Lyndon B. Johnson's ranch in Texas, this homemade barbecue sauce features common pantry items that will simmer into a delicious sauce before you can go to the store and buy a bottled version! I like to double the ingredients and save half for another day.

**TOTAL TIME:** 25 minutes
**MAKES:** about 3 cups      **SERVINGS:** 25, 2 tablespoons each
**TOTAL COST:** $1.88

## NUTRITIONAL INFORMATION

Calories: 25                Sodium: 243mg            Sugar: 6.9g
Total Fat: 0.1g             Carbohydrates: 7.3g      Protein: 0.1g
Saturated Fat: 0g           Fiber: 0.1g              Cholesterol: 0mg

## INGREDIENTS

1 cup no-sugar-added ketchup, such as Heinz Simply Ketchup
½ cup apple cider vinegar
1 ½ cups water
1 tablespoon brown sugar
1 teaspoon chili powder
1 tablespoon Worcestershire sauce

1 teaspoon paprika
⅛ teaspoon salt
⅛ teaspoon pepper
3 stalks celery, broken into 3 pieces each
¼ cup onion, roughly chopped
1 clove garlic, mashed
1 bay leaf

## DIRECTIONS

In a large saucepan, combine all of the ingredients. Bring to a boil and simmer over medium-low heat for 15 minutes. Strain in a fine mesh strainer. Serve with sandwiches or your favorite grilled cut of meat. Cool before refrigerating. Refrigerate for up to 1 month, or freeze for up to 3 months.

# SWEET GARLIC BBQ SAUCE

Sometimes I like a salty, tangy BBQ and other times I enjoy a sweeter sauce like this one. This sauce airs on the honey-BBQ side and has many layers of fresh flavor. It works great as a marinade or as a basting sauce. Put a dollop on your favorite sandwich or use as a dipping sauce for sweet potato or butternut squash fries.

**TOTAL TIME:** 5 minutes
**MAKES:** 1 ¾ cups     **SERVINGS:** 14, 2 tablespoons per serving
**TOTAL COST:** $2.19

## NUTRITIONAL INFORMATION

Calories: 46

Total Fat: 0g

Saturated Fat: 0g

Sodium: 183.4mg

Carbohydrates: 12.3g

Fiber: 0g

Sugar: 12g

Protein: 0.1g

Cholesterol: 0mg

## INGREDIENTS

1 cup no-sugar-added ketchup, such as Heinz Simply Ketchup
⅓ cup honey
2 teaspoons paprika
¼ cup apple cider vinegar
3 cloves of garlic, minced
2 dashes of garlic powder
Salt and pepper to season

## DIRECTIONS

Combine all ingredients in a small bowl. Whisk all ingredients together vigorously. Store in an airtight, sealed jar in the refrigerator for up to 2 weeks.

# ROASTED GARLIC

Looking for a low-calorie spread or a heart-healthy flavor booster? Simple roasted garlic is your new trick. Slather it on bread, toss it with green beans, mix it into dressings, or whip it into your favorite dip. It's simple, inexpensive, and tasty!

**PREP TIME:** 5 minutes    **BAKE TIME:** 40 minutes
**MAKES:** about ½ cup of roasted garlic
**SERVINGS:** 8, 1 tablespoon each
*TOTAL COST:* $1.50

## NUTRITIONAL INFORMATION

Calories: 25
Total Fat: 1.2g
Saturated Fat: 0.2g

Sodium: 50mg
Carbohydrates: 3.3g
Fiber: 0.2g

Sugar: 0.1g
Protein: 0.6g
Cholesterol: 0mg

## INGREDIENTS
5 large heads of garlic
1 tablespoon olive oil
¼ teaspoon salt

## DIRECTIONS

Preheat oven to 350°F. Cut the top portion of the garlic heads with a large prep knife to expose the cloves. Place the prepared heads on a sheet of tin foil and drizzle with the olive oil. Sprinkle with salt. Using the foil, wrap the garlic heads into a ball. Bake for 40 minutes. Cool completely.

Take each head and push the cloves out of the head with your fingers onto a cutting board. Sprinkle with a little salt. Use a fork to mash the roasted cloves into a paste. Use as desired. Store in an airtight container and refrigerate.

# USING YOUR ROASTED GARLIC

### ROASTED GARLIC GREEN BEANS

Clean and trim 1 pound of fresh green beans. Place in a large microwave-safe bowl and add 2 tablespoons of water. Cover tightly with plastic wrap and microwave for 3 minutes. Carefully remove the plastic wrap and drain the excess water. Toss green beans with 1 tablespoon olive oil, 1 tablespoon of roasted garlic, and salt and pepper.

### ROASTED GARLIC BRUSCHETTA

Slice 1 large baguette into ¼-inch slices. Lay out on a baking sheet and toast under the broiler in the oven for 30 seconds. Spread Roasted Garlic over the surface of the toasted baguette pieces and top with slices of Roma tomato, grated parmesan cheese, and freshly chopped basil.

### PARMESAN PEPPERCORN GARLIC DRESSING OR DIP

Combine the following items in a blender and blend until smooth:

> ¼ cup sour cream
> ¼ cup plain Greek yogurt
> ¼ cup light mayonnaise
> ¼ cup parmesan cheese
> 1 head of Roasted Garlic
> ¼ teaspoon freshly cracked black
>      pepper, or more if desired
> Salt to season

# DILLED RANCH DRESSING

Out of all the condiments on the market today, ranch dressing is the number-one favorite among my high school students. Every time we make dinner meals in class, I hear, "Mrs. K, can I have some ranch?" I swear those kids would dip brownies into ranch dressing. This homemade ranch dressing combines common ingredients from your refrigerator and pantry with some fresh herbs to make it tangy and yummy. Drizzle it on a lettuce wedge, dip some raw veggies into it . . . or slather it on your dessert if you dare. Well, maybe not.

**TOTAL TIME:** 7 minutes

**MAKES:** 1 ¾ cups  **SERVINGS:** 14, 2 tablespoons per serving

**TOTAL COST:** $2.45

## NUTRITIONAL INFORMATION

| | | |
|---|---|---|
| Calories: 40 | Sodium: 163mg | Sugar: 0.9g |
| Total Fat: 3.3g | Carbohydrates: 1.1g | Protein: 1.4g |
| Saturated Fat: 0.9g | Fiber: 0g | Cholesterol: 2.9mg |

## INGREDIENTS

½ cup light sour cream

½ cup light mayonnaise

½ cup nonfat plain Greek yogurt

1 tablespoon white or apple cider vinegar

1 tablespoon chopped fresh dill

2 tablespoons chopped chives or green onions

1 teaspoon Worcestershire sauce

½ teaspoon salt

½ teaspoon pepper

¼ teaspoon garlic powder

½ teaspoon paprika

## DIRECTIONS

Combine all ingredients in a small bowl. Whisk together vigorously. Store in an airtight sealed jar in the refrigerator for up to 1 week.

# GRAM BUCCI'S ITALIAN VINAIGRETTE

This dressing comes straight from the kitchen of my grandmother, Helen Bucci. This was the only dressing she ever served at her house for guests and everyone loved it. After she taught me how to make it, I've made it at least 3 times per week to accompany her standard romaine, cucumber, and tomato salad.

**TOTAL TIME:** 5 minutes

**MAKES:** ⅔ cup    **SERVINGS:** 4, 2 ½ tablespoons each

**TOTAL COST:** $0.91

### NUTRITIONAL INFORMATION

Calories: 65

Total Fat: 6.8g

Saturated Fat: 0.9g

Sodium: 382.5mg

Carbohydrates: 1g

Fiber: 0g

Sugar: 1g

Protein: 0g

Cholesterol: 0mg

### INGREDIENTS

¼ cup extra virgin olive oil

¼ cup red wine vinegar

¼ cup balsamic vinegar

2 teaspoons Nature Seasoning (found in your spice aisle with a blue cap)

### DIRECTIONS

In a small bowl, whisk together all ingredients until thoroughly mixed. Pour over the salad and serve immediately. Refrigerate in a sealed container for up to 2 weeks.

## DRESSING STORAGE TIP

To save on refrigerator space and Tupperware costs, reuse an empty, thoroughly washed dressing or condiment bottle. Use a funnel to pour the prepared dressing or sauce into the bottle. Label the container and store in the refrigerator.

# CREAMY POPPY SEED DRESSING

This dressing pairs best with sweet ingredients in salads, such as berries, pears, and oranges. It also makes a good sweet slaw dressing over broccoli slaw and shredded cabbage.

**PREP TIME:** 5 minutes
**MAKES:** ⅔ cup   **SERVINGS:** 5, 2 tablespoons each
*TOTAL COST:* $1.10

## NUTRITIONAL INFORMATION

Calories: 77

Total Fat: 4g

Saturated Fat: 0.5g

Sodium: 78.4mg

Carbohydrates: 9.8g

Fiber: 0.2g

Sugar: 8.8g

Protein: 0.9g

Cholesterol: 4mg

## INGREDIENTS

¼ cup light mayonnaise

2 tablespoons plain Greek yogurt

1 tablespoon poppy seeds

3 tablespoons sugar

2 tablespoons red wine vinegar

Salt and pepper to season

## DIRECTIONS

In a small bowl, whisk together the light mayonnaise, Greek yogurt, poppy seeds, sugar, and red wine vinegar. Season the dressing with salt and pepper to taste. Serve or refrigerate in a sealed container for up to 2 weeks.

# CAESAR DRESSING

This is my take on a classic Caesar dressing, but without the raw egg yolk. It dresses a chicken salad beautifully, but also serves as a good room-temperature sauce over asparagus and pasta salad.

**TOTAL TIME:** 5 minutes
**MAKES:** ½ cup    **SERVINGS:** 6, 1 ½ tablespoons each
*TOTAL COST:* $1.28

## NUTRITIONAL INFORMATION

Calories: 92
Total Fat: 9.5g
Saturated Fat: 1.2g

Sodium: 174.8mg
Carbohydrates: 0.9g
Fiber: 0.1g

Sugar: 0.2g
Protein: 0.6g
Cholesterol: 0mg

## INGREDIENTS

Juice of 1 lemon
1 tablespoon Dijon mustard
1 clove garlic, finely minced and smashed into a paste with the back of your knife
1 tablespoon anchovy paste (optional)
4 tablespoons extra virgin olive oil, divided
Salt and freshly ground black pepper to season

## DIRECTIONS

In a small bowl, combine the lemon juice, Dijon mustard, garlic clove, and anchovy paste with a small whisk. Whisk in 4 tablespoons olive oil until completely combined. Season dressing with salt and pepper to taste. Use immediately or store in a sealed container for up to 1 week.

# HONEY MUSTARD DRESSING

This sweet and tangy dressing pairs well with savory salads, but it also makes a great marinade and basting sauce for grilled meat. I even use it as a dip for raw veggies.

**TOTAL TIME:** 5 minutes
**MAKES:** ⅔ cup   **SERVINGS:** 5, 2 tablespoons each
**TOTAL COST:** $1.48

## NUTRITIONAL INFORMATION

Calories: 110
Total Fat: 5.4g
Saturated Fat: 0.7g

Sodium: 358.5mg
Carbohydrates: 12.9g
Fiber: 0.1g

Sugar: 13.8g
Protein: 0.1g
Cholesterol: 0mg

## INGREDIENTS
¼ cup honey
¼ cup Dijon mustard
2 tablespoons olive oil
Salt and pepper to season

## DIRECTIONS

In a small bowl, combine the honey, Dijon mustard, and olive oil. Whisk vigorously. Season with salt and pepper and whisk again until the dressing is thoroughly combined. Serve or refrigerate in a sealed container for up to 2 weeks.

# THOUSAND ISLAND DRESSING

It's difficult to find a bottled light Thousand Island dressing that tastes this good. You can whip this up very quickly for your Reuben sandwiches for under $1!

**TOTAL TIME:** 5 minutes
**MAKES:** ¾ cup     **SERVINGS:** 6, 2 tablespoons each
**TOTAL COST:** $0.50

## NUTRITIONAL INFORMATION

Calories: 41

Total Fat: 2.7g

Saturated Fat: 0.3g

Sodium: 253.9mg

Carbohydrates: 4.2g

Fiber: 0.1g

Sugar: 3.5g

Protein: 0.1g

Cholesterol: 3.3mg

## INGREDIENTS

¼ cup light mayonnaise
¼ cup no-sugar-added ketchup, such as Heinz Simply Ketchup
3 tablespoons pickles, minced
1 tablespoon pickle juice
1 dash of garlic powder
Salt and pepper to season

## DIRECTIONS

In a small bowl, whisk together all ingredients until well combined. Serve or refrigerate in an airtight container for up to 2 weeks.

# ASIAN VINAIGRETTE

I love to order a house salad at hibachi restaurants just for the sake of the amazing dressing—it tastes so different from any bottled dressing on the market today. This is my take on that unique sauce. Feel free to eliminate the peanut butter if desired.

**TOTAL TIME:** 7 minutes

**MAKES:** ⅞ cup    **SERVINGS:** 7, 2 tablespoons each

**TOTAL COST:** $1.82

## NUTRITIONAL INFORMATION

Calories: 110

Total Fat: 10.1g

Saturated Fat: 1.5g

Sodium: 198.1mg

Carbohydrates: 4.5g

Fiber: 0.3g

Sugar: 3.3g

Protein: 1.4g

Cholesterol: 0mg

## INGREDIENTS

2 tablespoons low-sodium soy sauce

2 tablespoons rice wine vinegar

2 tablespoons peanut butter

2 tablespoons orange juice

1 tablespoon honey

1 clove garlic, minced

¼ cup sesame oil

1 teaspoon grated ginger (optional)

Salt and pepper to season

## DIRECTIONS

In a blender, combine all ingredients and puree until smooth. Season with salt and pepper as desired. Store in an airtight container for up to 1 week.